For my mom. There are so many things I have wanted to tell you.

Published in 2008 by Stewart, Tabori & Chang
An imprint of Harry N. Abrams, Inc.

Library of Congress Cataloging-in-Publication Data
Bernard, Wendy.
  Custom knits : Unleash Your Inner Designer with Top-Down and
Improvisational Techniques / by Wendy Bernard.
    p. cm.
  "STC Craft/A Melanie Falick book."
  ISBN 978-1-58479-713-5
  1. Knitting—Patterns. 2. Sweaters. I. Title.

TT825.B396 2008
746.43'2041—dc22

                      2007042698

Editors: Melanie Falick and Liana Allday
Designer: Anna Christian
Production Manager: Jacqueline Poirier

The text of this book was composed in Pastonchi and Sassoon.

Printed and bound in China
10 9 8 7 6 5 4 3 2 1

HNA
harry n. abrams, inc.
a subsidiary of La Martinière Groupe
115 West 18th Street
New York, NY 10011
www.hnabooks.com

custom knits

Unleash Your Inner Designer with Top-Down and Improvisational Techniques

Wendy Bernard *photographs by Kimball Hall*
photostyling by Mark Auria

STC Craft | A Melanie Falick Book ◆ New York

CONTENTS

INTRODUCTION

My knitting story began when I made my first project, a baby hat. Soon after, I made a baby sweater, and then a sweater for myself—a nifty long-sleeved pullover in an acrylic blend. I spent many hours knitting and many more seaming, but when I finished it and pulled it over my head, I discovered, to my horror, that it didn't fit, and the shoulder seams looked awful. Even though I was bewildered by the end result, my passion for knitting—and collecting yarn and pattern books—continued to build.

Since those early days I have become acquainted with hundreds of knitters—probably thousands if I count those I have "met" in cyberspace—and I've come to find that my experiences aren't unique. It seems like, for most of us, knitting has its ups and downs. You know, the big rise, and then—at times—the big fall when we realize that the creamy yellow yarn we chose with so much care isn't flattering against our complexion, or that the turtleneck that looked so fab on the model in the picture is really too bulky for our bodies. But over time (and many knitted sweaters), I have figured out some easy ways to avoid many of these disappointments. They involve both preplanning—understanding how to evaluate what really looks good on *me* rather than a model—and sensitive, customized construction. That is to say, knowing how to adapt a pattern to suit my personal style and fit needs. I call this unleashing my inner designer.

When I first started knitting I always worked my sweaters in pieces—a front, a back, and two sleeves—seaming those pieces together at the end of the process. That's what the patterns told me to do and I honestly didn't know there was any other way to do it. Thing is, I found seaming difficult to do well and I also had trouble figuring out how to customize the pieces so they would fit together perfectly. But then one day I discovered that sweaters could be knit from the top down and in one piece, which basically means you start working the front and back at the top of the sweater, connect them when you get below the armholes, and then work in the round down to the hem. Sleeves are added next and are worked in the round from the shoulder to the cuffs. And then a collar of your choice can be added on last. Knitting this way allows you to try on as you go, change your mind in the process, and essentially design on the fly. Because you're picking up stitches at the shoulder and working down, you can add sleeves

to a garment that you thought would be a shell. You can lengthen or add shaping to an otherwise boxy sweater, or change the look of a collar entirely, with only a little bit of know-how. And because you're working the front and back at the same time on a circular needle, all of your design elements and shaping happen at the same time, so you don't need to take meticulous notes and remember exactly what you did on one piece in order to mimic it on another—maybe a month later. And the best thing is, except for weaving in some loose ends, there's little to no seaming, so after binding off your last stitch, your sweater is pretty much complete. Amazing, right?

I learned these techniques from a variety of sources but was most significantly influenced by the work of two brilliant women: Elizabeth Zimmermann and Barbara Walker. Zimmermann's no-nonsense approach to knitting, in particular circular knitting and making sweaters without an "official" pattern, inspired me to be the boss of my own craft and look at knitting much more improvisationally. Walker, on the other hand, introduced me to techniques for knitting from the top down—a form of sweater construction that allowed me to knit to my exact specifications, and that made knitting sweaters fun and easy. In fact, it was the work of both Zimmermann and Walker that inspired me to begin designing patterns on my own. I became so excited by what I was doing that I shared my experiences and patterns on my blog called Knit and Tonic (knitandtonic. net). The response was so positive—this information was helping others develop confidence in their own skills and creativity—that it led me to write this book.

I've divided *Custom Knits* into six sections. In Chapter 1, I share what I've learned about figuring out what to knit based on what is flattering to our figures and what fits into our lifestyles. For instance, I may be tempted now and then to make myself a bulky alpine ski sweater, but considering I live in Southern California and don't ski, a cotton shell might get a bit more wear in my wardrobe. Chapter 1 also covers the basics of interpreting a pattern, especially a schematic, so we can really "see" what the garment is going to look like and how it's going to fit (photos in patterns, as you've likely noticed, can sometimes be misleading). This kind of preplanning helps us to decide if we want to knit the garment as is, or unleash our inner designers and customize. I also share what I've learned about taking measurements and give instructions for making one's very own dress form using duct tape that mimics one's real figure so instead of trying on as we go, our dress form can try on for us and we can see how our work is progressing from all angles.

Chapters 2 through 5 are dedicated to patterns: top-down raglan sweaters, top-down set-in sleeve sweaters, bottom-up round-yoke sweaters, and patterns to design on the fly. Because top-down knitting and improvisational techniques have been so life-altering for me and my knitting happiness, I have designed almost every sweater in this book to be constructed in this fashion. The patterns come in a wide range of sizes (x-small to 3x-large) and can be worked exactly as written, but each pattern also comes with ideas to get you started on customization. In many cases, I even show you variations I've made to my own patterns. The designing on the fly chapter features very simple patterns I created by using existing favorite garments or simple calculations and stitch patterns, and almost no seaming.

Finally, for those of you who want to get serious about customizing your garments, at the end of the book I've included a reference section of helpful techniques, including an overview of sweater elements that can be altered, and formulas for how to design a sweater from scratch with no pattern at all. Read about these techniques as you go and before you know it, you'll be looking at patterns in a new way. Rather than seeing the designer's choices as hard and fast, you'll see them as jumping-off points for your own creations. You'll no longer need to search for that "perfect" pattern, the one that you've been looking for and looking for and looking for. *That* pattern probably doesn't exist. But if you apply some of these improvisational techniques to preexisting patterns, you'll be able to create your own "perfect" pattern. And in doing so, you're likely to discover a whole new knitting experience, one that will help you make the leap from fantasy knitting to reality knitting, which I think is much more satisfying, and will give you confidence and a new outlook on your skills.

Wendy.

CHAPTER 1

Understanding Your Style, Size, and Fit So You Can Make Sweaters You Love to Wear

I know a lot of people who knit sweaters just to knit them. They're passionate about the process but consider the result a crap shoot. Maybe they will look great, maybe not. I used to be like that but now that I've acquired some basic skills, I feel confident when I cast on that I'm going to be thrilled when I bind off. This chapter is all about pinpointing the styles that really work for you, figuring out your size, and then evaluating the pattern in order to be able to visualize what the final result will look like on your body. Once you understand these basic concepts, you're well on your way to successfully creating flattering sweaters that you'll love to wear.

FINDING STYLES THAT WORK

I have knit piles of sweaters and, I'll be honest, the ones that get the most wear are near copies of some of the store-bought ones I have neatly folded in my drawers—ones that I have sort of road-tested and know that I'll make use of. For example, the Favorite Sweater on page 126: I used a favorite and well-loved store-bought sweater as a guide when I designed it. Why? Because I wore the store-bought one so much that I literally wore it out, and the only way to reclaim it was to design and knit one like it. Sure, it's not in the same gauge and doesn't have wall-to-wall cables like my store-bought one, but it has similar lines and a similar look—and it's in the same color. And, it looks good on me and works well with my wardrobe. This same rule often applies to my yarn choice. For instance, I may love the sumptuous feel of alpaca, but breathable fibers like linen and cotton are often much more appropriate for my California climate.

Far too often we dream-knitters look through pattern books and lose sight of what we know we'd be most likely to wear. We spot a pattern that looks so gorgeous, that's so sumptuous or whatever it is that draws us in, and forget that the model who's wearing the sweater has been styled and groomed just for this particular sweater. Not to mention, she's 5'9" and we are maybe 5'4", or that her particular shape welcomes an allover ribbed pattern . . . and ours? (You can fill in the blank.)

Still, knitting should be fun. We should be allowed to dream. We should be allowed to fantasize about the finished project and how it's going to change our lives, although I'll make a suggestion: Make a reality checklist before you purchase the yarn. The pattern? Purchase the pattern if you like it; buy the book if you want to. But before you commit to the yarn, work through My Reality Checklist on the facing page to evaluate if the pattern will work for you as is, or if you need to make some adjustments (and if even then it will be right for you). Deep down we usually know what suits us, even when that beautiful model is staring back at us and cooing "Knit me, NOW."

My Reality Checklist:
Never Leave Home Without It

STYLE

✦ Does this style fit into my lifestyle? Will I have many opportunities to wear this garment?

✦ Does this style work with my body type? Would I have to lose a few pounds to wear it? Is this a realistic or healthy ambition?

✦ Is this a style that I can wear for more than one season? Do I care?

✦ Is this style trendy and splashed all over the fashion pages? Do I care? Will I be able to finish the garment before it looks outdated?

✦ Will I have to wear special undergarments to make it work?

✦ What, if any, changes do I need to make to the style to make it truly work for me?

FIT

✦ Does this style flatter my body? If not, what kinds of changes do I need to make so it will?

✦ How does the finished size compare to my actual body measurements? What does that tell me about how it will fit?

GAUGE

✦ Do I look good in this weight of yarn? (This is an especially important question when considering working with bulky yarn.)

✦ Do I have the time and fortitude it takes to finish a sweater in a really small gauge?

✦ To achieve this gauge, do I need to use needles that hurt my hands? Will I complain so much that my friends and those close to me will beg me to stop knitting it?

YARN

✦ Is the yarn called for available?

✦ Is it affordable?

✦ Will it feel good on my body?

✦ Is it practical? Can it be laundered? Will it work in my climate? Do I care?

✦ Is the color shown one I enjoy wearing? If I change the color, will the garment still have the same look?

✦ Can I substitute another yarn for the one called for in the pattern and retain the overall look of the garment in the photo?

✦ If I have a yarn in my stash I really want to use, but it "just might work," do I really want to plow ahead? Or should I bite the bullet and buy yarn that I know will work so I end up with a garment I really like?

SHOES

✦ Will I be forced to buy new shoes to go with it? (The preferred answer is yes.)

Now think about your answers. If you still feel excited, it's time to gather your yarn. If you've determined that this is not a garment you will wear but you still want to make it, see if you can think of someone else for whom you'd enjoy knitting it.

CHOOSING YARN WISELY

Typically, a designer will select yarn based on a couple of factors, like how it will drape and how it will show a particular stitch pattern. If you use the specified yarn, you will turn out a sweater that comes the closest to resembling the one you see in the picture. But if you substitute another yarn—especially if you are swapping it for a different fiber altogether—there's a lot more to consider than gauge, including texture, fiber content, and weight.

For starters, examine the pattern and look for the weight of the specified yarn. For example, let's say you would like to knit a pattern whose selected yarn has a gauge of 5 stitches per inch and 260 yards to 100 grams, and you are considering swapping it out for some yarn with the same gauge that has 110 yards to 50 grams. If you divide the number of grams by the number of yards, you'll know that the selected yarn's weight is 0.38 grams per yard and the one you want to swap it for is 0.45 grams per yard. Armed with the knowledge that your subbed yarn is heavier, you can still expect your garment, once finished, will have the same shape and the correct size, but will it have the same drape and body? Probably not. The closer your subbed yarn is to the selected one in terms of its texture, fiber content, and weight, the more likely it is that your garment will look like the one in the picture. Note that if you plan on making changes to the pattern, you may need more yarn than the pattern calls for. See Determining How Much Yarn to Buy (page 160) for more information.

WHAT SIZE AM I ANYWAY?

Let's be honest: Half the battle of carrying off a knitted item is in our attitude. For example, if one of us is wearing a so-so knitted item with a great big bunch of confidence, no one else seems to notice that we dropped a stitch, miscrossed one of the cables, or ran out of yarn and had to finish the collar and pockets with yarn from a different dye lot. In fact, I'll venture to say that if any of us is wearing something on the verge of average but with the right amount of attitude, we're looking great.

But fit is something else altogether. If we're wearing an ill-fitting item, it's not so much that other people notice. *We* notice. There is nothing worse than wearing a sweater that doesn't hang right, that hangs too low, is too short, or is just plain uncomfortable. As perfect as this garment might be otherwise, our personal discomfort shows through. So, to be sure we're knitting a size that will fit, we knitters first need to know our measurements.

Taking Measurements—With a Little Help From Our Friends

Although most of us can take our own measurements, the contortions required may impact our results. So, to get accurate numbers, ask a friend to come on over and help.

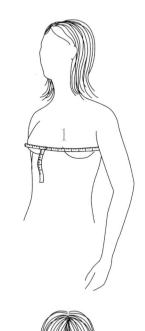

1 **Chest/Bust:** Measure around the fullest part of your chest. Unless you're built like a Barbie doll, wear a decent foundation garment, but not one with tons of padding or tassels.

2 **Center Back Neck-to-Cuff:** With arm bent slightly, measure from the back base of your neck across your shoulder and around the bend of your elbow. This is useful when working saddle-shoulder sweaters and can be used if you want to make a sweater that is knit from cuff to cuff.

3 **Back Waist Length:** For this measurement, measure from the base of your neck to what you consider to be your natural waistline. This is an especially helpful measurement when it comes to top-down knitting. If you know where the back waist is supposed to be in a pattern, you can time your waist shaping so that the smallest circumference of the sweater lands where it should. (But then, trying on as you go—which is something I encourage—takes all the guesswork away.)

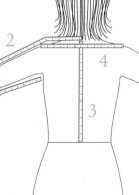

4 **Crossback:** Measure from one shoulder to another, but stop where the top bump of your shoulders are. Think of a well-fitting suit and consider where the armhole/sleeve seam would lie. Measure between those two points. This is an ultra-important measurement. Why? If you knit a sweater with a too-wide crossback measurement, then the sleeves will not sit in the correct position and the width of the back will be too wide.

5 **Sleeve Length:** Measure from your armpit down to your wrist, bending your arm slightly. Note that there isn't a hard and fast rule saying that your sweater sleeve must be the same length as your personal measurement. For example, there will be times when you want to add length for a turned up cuff or for a bit of extra sass and style.

READING SCHEMATICS

Let's all go ahead and look at our new favorite pattern. Let's ooh and ahh and get it all out of our systems. Honestly. Take a moment or two.

Now that that's over with, what's the next step? Go and grab yarn? Nope. This is where the hard part starts. Knitting? That's easy compared to this, because now is the time to look at the picture, compare it to the schematic, compare the schematic to our bodies, factor in our likes and dislikes and shape requirements, and sum it all up.

I wrote this book, I designed the garments in it, and I knit almost every one before meeting the model who would be wearing it in the photo. I didn't know her size, her arm length, or anything else before I knit the sample. We were able to choose models we thought would fit in the sweaters and we had stylists and makeup artists—Hollywood magic—on hand to make the pictures look gorgeous. On top of all of that, the models are trained to lean so that the garments hang "just so." *That* is why schematics are so important. Never mind what you see on the model. Look at the schematic. Look at the yarn. Look at the gauge. If the model appears to be wearing a shaped sweater and the schematic shows straight lines along the sides of the body, the schematic trumps the picture. These are the clues that will give you the whole picture and a clear idea about how your project will turn out, and whether or not you will want to make some adjustments.

So what exactly is a schematic and what will it do for you? It's a flat illustration with measurements at key points. It's meant to explain the actual shape of the garment: length, width at various points, armhole measurement, sleeve length, back measurement, and hopefully everything else you need to know about its intended dimensions.

If you know your actual body measurements and take a look at the finished measurements on a schematic, you will be able to decide if the size you are choosing will fit the way you want it to fit, and if enough ease will be built into the garment (see the facing page for more information on ease). Do you have a sleeve measurement of 19" yet the one shown in the schematic is 17"? Then you'll want to add 2" to what the pattern calls for (and make sure you have enough yarn [see page 160]). Is your waist nearly the same measurement as your bust, and does the schematic show an extremely shaped waist? Then you might want to omit a shaping round or two when you are working that section.

UNDERSTANDING EASE

When designers create a garment, they know how they want it to fit the wearer, so they build it around standard measurements plus or minus "ease" (additional or fewer inches or centimeters). Standard is a relative term and each designer might have his or her own ideas about ease, but we have to start somewhere, so let's start with the recommendations issued by the Craft Yarn Council of America (www.yarnstandards.com), which I know a lot of handknit designers follow. The inch/cm measurements represent how much fabric is added (or taken away) to achieve the desired fit.

Very close-fitting:	Actual chest/bust measurement or less
Close-fitting:	1-2"/2.5-5 cm
Standard-fitting:	2-4"/5-10 cm
Loose-fitting:	4-6"/10-15 cm
Oversized:	6"/15 cm or more

So, when you look at a pattern, take a look at the finished measurements, either in the beginning of the instructions or on the schematic. Compare these measurements to your own actual measurements to determine how much ease there will really be if you follow the pattern for your "usual" size. For example, if the finished bust measurement is 6" larger than your actual bust measurement, then you know the garment will fit loosely, at least in that area of your body. On the other hand, if the finished bust measurement is 1" smaller than your actual bust measurement (called negative ease), then the garment will be very close fitting across the bust.

DRESS FORMS

A good way to make sure your garments will fit you is to use a dress form. Not only will it eliminate the need for you to remove your clothing every time you want to try on your garment, it will also give you an opportunity to see how your garment really looks from all sides. While you can definitely buy a dress form—even one with dials that you can adjust to match your main body measurements—it really isn't necessary if you're up for making your own out of duct tape and have a good friend around willing to help (see pages 18-19).

Make Me a Double!

Here is a quick and easy way to make an inexpensive dress form. Once the process starts, you will want to move quickly. Have all the materials at the ready, and whatever you do, don't strike a pose. When I made my first one, I did, and now I have a dress form with the right hip jutted out "just so."

1 Don your old T-shirt (you will cut it up later, so make sure it is disposable); wear your normal underwear/bra underneath. Stand naturally but straight, feet a couple of inches apart, and have your helper begin by wrapping varying lengths of tape horizontally at the bottom, around the lower-hip level, overlapping the tape. Have him or her wrap it firmly but not so tight that it acts like a girdle. On this first layer, when you reach the waist area, ask the helper to wrap a little looser, and contour it to your waist. Folds may appear, but this is normal.

2 Work up to the bust and the underarm, allowing the tape to follow your figure. Wrap a length of plastic wrap around your neck to protect it. At this point, you may need to cut the T-shirt sleeves, leaving 1" of T-shirt hanging out past the duct tape. When you are ready to tape around the armholes and neckline, fold the duct tape over the cut sleeve edges—and on the neckline, around the plastic—making firm, rounded edges. Arrange shorter pieces of tape in a radial fashion over the bust. Encourage some "cross your heart" action to emphasize your shape. Continue using shorter pieces of tape and work to the tops of the shoulders.

3 Do another full layer, this time placing the pieces of tape vertically over the body. Then do a third layer, wrapping the lengths of tape horizontally, like the first layer, and compressing the waistline to fit the layers of duct tape underneath more closely. Make sure to smooth over any wrinkles.

4 When you are satisfied, bend over slightly, have a sip of your beverage, and ask your helper to draw a line with a permanent marker where your waistline creases. If you want, ask your helper to mark the center point of your chest, as well as any other notations you think are necessary, such as the date.

5 Ask your helper to carefully cut the form and T-shirt (the tape will stick to the T-shirt) off of you at the center back, making sure to cut through layers of tape and T-shirt only, avoiding your bra underneath.

6 Close up the form with additional tape, except for the top of the neck. Place a sturdy hanger inside, and tape up the rest of the neck and back.

7 Stuff the form completely with fiberfill. Cut a piece of cardboard to fit the bottom of the form and tape it in place so the batting doesn't fall out.

8 After you have recovered from the shock of what your body really looks like (I always thought I was narrower in the waist and had a larger chest), name your form and hang it in a closet. You can pull it out whenever you are knitting a garment or feel the urge to try something on without trying it on. If you happen to be knitting a garment in pieces—which I hardly ever do—you will have to pin each piece directly on the form to see the fit. If this is the case, find an old pillowcase or a few yards of jersey and wrap it around the form or pin it on. You can easily push pins through the fabric without damaging the duct tape.

CHAPTER 2

Top-Down Raglan Sweaters

Raglan sweaters, whether knit from the top down, bottom up, in the round, or in separate pattern pieces, have the distinction of sporting diagonal shaping lines that run from the top of the shoulder down to the underarm. Some people claim raglans are one-trick ponies—meaning they sort of always look the same—but I enjoy dispelling that idea. All of the raglans in this section are knit from the top down and in the round and are started at the collar or at the neck. And guess what? Most of them have minimal finishing, so when you bind off your last stitch you will have practically finished your sweater. If you are new to top-down raglans, check out Pink on page 22 to learn the basics.

SIZES

X-Small (Small, Medium, Large,
1X-Large, 2X-Large, 3X-Large)

FINISHED MEASUREMENTS

29¼ (33, 35½, 39, 43½, 48,
50¾)" chest

YARN

Lana Grossa New Cotton
(60% cotton / 40% microfiber;
153 yards / 50 grams): 5 (6, 7,
7, 8, 10, 10) balls #007 (MC);
1 ball #013 (A)

NEEDLES

One 29" (74 cm) long or longer
circular (circ) needle size US 8
(5 mm)

One 29" (74 cm) long or longer
circ needle size US 6 (4 mm)

One or two 24" (60 cm) long or
longer circ needles or one set of
five double-pointed needles (dpn)
size US 8 (5 mm), as preferred,
for Sleeves

One or two 24" (60 cm) long or
longer circ needles or one set of
five dpn size US 6 (4 mm), as
preferred, for Sleeves

Change needle size if necessary
to obtain correct gauge.

NOTIONS

Stitch markers; waste yarn

GAUGE

18 sts and 28 rows = 4" (10 cm)
in Stockinette stitch (St st) using
larger needles

PINK

Pink is by far the most basic raglan-style garment in this book. This one
is fitted and features an optional stripe sequence on one of the sleeves.
Even though the top-down raglan isn't the simplest of all the types of
top-down or one-piece garments you can make, it is one that seems to be
most familiar to knitters. The nice thing about top-down raglans is that
they seem, at least to me, to be the easiest of all forms on which to base
a new pattern. In other words, if you know how to construct one of these,
a whole new world of potential design adaptations will open up to you.

PATTERN FEATURES
Top-down raglan construction, body and sleeves worked in the round,
simple color changes

STITCH PATTERNS

1×1 Rib in-the-Round
(multiple of 2 sts; 1-rnd repeat)
All Rnds: *K1, p1; repeat from * around.

1×1 Rib
(multiple of 2 sts; 1-row repeat)
Row 1 (WS): P1, *k1, p1; repeat from * to end.
Row 2: Knit the knit sts and purl the purl sts as they face you.
Repeat Row 2 for 1×1 Rib.

YOKE

With larger 29″ long circ needle, CO 1 st for Right Front, place marker (pm), 4 (4, 4, 4, 6, 6, 6) sts for Right Sleeve, pm, 20 (24, 26, 30, 30, 30, 34) sts for Back, pm, 4 (4, 4, 4, 6, 6, 6) sts for Left Sleeve, pm, and 1 st for Left Front—30 (34, 36, 40, 44, 44, 48) sts.

Next Row (RS): [K1-f/b, slip marker (sm), k1-f/b, work to 1 st before next marker] 3 times, k1-f/b, sm, k1-f/b—38 (42, 44, 48, 52, 52, 56) sts. Purl 1 row.

Shape Raglan (RS): Increase 8 sts this row, then every other row 20 (21, 22, 23, 28, 31, 32) times, as follows: [Work to 1 st before next marker, k1-f/b, sm, k1-f/b] 4 times, work to end, and AT THE SAME TIME, on next RS row,

Shape Neck (RS): Continuing raglan shaping as established, increase 1 st at beginning and end of this row, every 4 rows 8 (10, 11, 10, 10, 10, 10) times, then every other row 0 (0, 0, 3, 3, 3, 4) times—224 (240, 252, 268, 312, 336, 350) sts.

BODY

Next Row (RS): Work across 32 (35, 37, 40, 45, 48, 50) sts of Right Front, transfer next 48 (50, 52, 54, 66, 72, 74) sts to waste yarn for Right Sleeve, removing markers, CO 1 (2, 3, 4, 4, 6, 6) sts for underarm, pm for side, CO 1 (2, 3, 4, 4, 6, 6) sts for underarm, work across 64 (70, 74, 80, 90, 96, 102) sts of Back, transfer next 48 (50, 52, 54, 66, 72, 74) sts to waste yarn for Left Sleeve, removing markers, CO 1 (2, 3, 4, 4, 6, 6) sts for underarm, pm for beginning of rnd, CO 1 (2, 3, 4, 4, 6, 6) sts for underarm—132 (148, 160, 176, 196, 216, 226) sts. Join for working in the rnd. Begin St st (knit every rnd). Work even for 14 (14, 14, 16, 16, 16, 16) rnds.

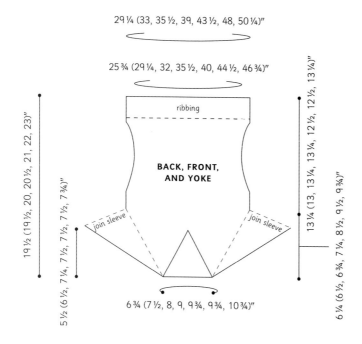

29 ¼ (33, 35 ½, 39, 43 ½, 48, 50 ¼)″

25 ¾ (29 ¼, 32, 35 ½, 40, 44 ½, 46 ¾)″

ribbing

BACK, FRONT, AND YOKE

19 ½ (19 ½, 20, 20 ½, 21, 22, 23)″

5 ½ (6 ½, 7 ¼, 7 ½, 7 ½, 7 ¾)″

join sleeve

join sleeve

13 ¼ (13, 13 ¼, 13 ¼, 12 ½, 12 ½, 13 ¼)″

6 ¼ (6 ½, 6 ¾, 7 ¼, 8 ½, 9 ½, 9 ¾)″

6 ¾ (7 ½, 8, 9, 9 ¾, 9 ¾, 10 ¾)″

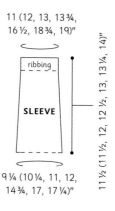

11 (12, 13, 13 ¾, 16 ½, 18 ¾, 19)″

ribbing

SLEEVE

11 ½ (11 ½, 12, 12 ½, 13, 13 ¼, 14)″

9 ¼ (10 ¼, 11, 12, 14 ¾, 17, 17 ¼)″

Shape Waist: Decrease 4 sts this rnd, then every 7 rnds 3 times, as follows: K1, k2tog, work to 3 sts before next marker, ssk, k1, sm, k1, k2tog, work to last 3 sts, k1, ssk—116 (132, 144, 160, 180, 200, 210) sts remain. Work even for 7 rnds.

Increase Rnd: Increase 4 sts this rnd, then every 7 rnds 3 times, as follows: K1, m1, work to 1 st before next marker, m1, k1, sm, k1, m1, work to last st, m1, k1—132 (148, 160, 176, 196, 216, 226) sts. Work even until piece measures 17 (17, 17½, 18, 18½, 19½, 20½)" from the beginning.

Next Rnd: Change to smaller circ needle and 1×1 Rib in-the-Round. Work even for 2½". BO all sts loosely in pattern.

SLEEVES

Note: Use your preferred method of working in the rnd when working the Sleeves (see page 150).

Transfer Sleeve sts from waste yarn to larger needle(s). With RS facing, join yarn at underarm; begin St st, work to end, pick up and knit 1 (2, 3, 4, 4, 6, 6) sts from sts CO for underarm, pm for beginning of rnd, pick up and knit 1 (2, 3, 4, 4, 6, 6) sts from sts CO for underarm—50 (54, 58, 62, 74, 84, 86) sts. Join for working in the rnd; work even for 6 rnds.

Shape Sleeve: Decrease 2 sts this rnd, then every 7 rnds 3 times, as follows: K1, k2tog, work to last 3 sts, ssk, k1—42 (46, 50, 54, 66, 76, 78) sts remain, and AT THE SAME TIME,

Begin Stripes: Change to A. Continuing Sleeve shaping as established, work even for 4 rnds. Change to MC. *Work even for 2 rnds. Change to A. Work even for 4 rnds. Repeat from * once.

Next Rnd: Change to MC. Work even until Sleeve measures 10 (10, 10½, 11, 11½, 11¾, 12½)" from underarm, or to 1½" less than desired length.

Next Rnd: Change to smaller needle(s) and 1×1 Rib. Work even for 1½". BO all sts loosely in pattern.

FINISHING
Neckband

With RS facing, using smaller 24" circ needle and MC, pick up and knit approximately 2 sts for every 3 rows along Right Front, 1 st in every CO st along top of Sleeves and Back, and approximately 2 sts for every 3 rows along Left Front, ending with an even number of sts.

Next Row (WS): Working back and forth, begin 1×1 Rib. Work even until ribbing measures 1½", or to desired length. *Note: For larger sizes, you may want to add a few extra rnds of ribbing before binding off.* BO all sts loosely in pattern. Sew lower right-hand edge of Neckband to bottom left-hand edge of neckline; sew lower left-hand edge of Neckband to bottom right-hand edge of neckline, behind right-hand edge of Neckband.

Block as desired.

MAKE IT YOUR OWN

Obviously, you can make fewer or more stripes, or none at all. For a more plunging neckline, work more rows even between increases when working the neck shaping for the Yoke. When you have added all your Front stitches, join the body together and continue working as instructed.

SIZES

X-Small (Small, Medium, Large,
1X-Large, 2X-Large, 3X-Large)

FINISHED MEASUREMENTS

33¼ (37, 40½, 44, 48½, 52,
55½)" chest

YARN

Blue Sky Alpacas Dyed Cotton
(100% organically grown cotton;
150 yards / 100 grams): 8 (8,
9, 10, 11, 12, 12) hanks #624
indigo

NEEDLES

One 29" (74 cm) long or longer
circular (circ) needle size US 7
(4.5 mm)

One or two 24" (60 cm) long or
longer circ needles or one set of
five double-pointed needles (dpn)
size US 7 (4.5 mm), as preferred,
for Sleeves

Change needle size if necessary
to obtain correct gauge.

NOTIONS

Stitch markers in 2 different
colors; removable markers;
waste yarn

GAUGE

18 sts and 22 rows = 4" (10 cm)
in Stockinette stitch (St st)

INDIGO PLAYMATE JACKET

Fashioned after the traditional gentleman's smoking jacket, this is the sort of sweater that can go from frump to fashionable in two shakes of the hip. Since it is knit from the top down and all in one piece, knitting is a breeze. Although it is worked in pure cotton, you could easily substitute wool or some other blend to make it even warmer and more wonderful, as long as the gauge stays the same.

PATTERN FEATURES
Top-down raglan construction, sleeves worked in the round, short-row shaping

STITCH PATTERNS

2×2 Rib

(multiple of 4 sts + 2; 1-row repeat)

Row 1 (RS): K2, *p2, k2; repeat from * to end.

Row 2: Knit the knit sts and purl the purl sts as they face you.

Repeat Row 2 for 2×2 Rib.

2×2 Rib in-the-Round

(multiple of 4 sts; 1-rnd repeat)

All Rnds: *K2, p2; repeat from * around.

YOKE

With 29″ long circ needle, CO 1 st for Left Front, place marker (pm), 4 (4, 4, 4, 5, 5, 5) sts for Left Sleeve, pm, 22 (24, 26, 28, 28, 30, 34) sts for Back, pm, 4 (4, 4, 4, 5, 5, 5) sts for Right Sleeve, pm, and 1 st for Right Front—32 (34, 36, 38, 40, 42, 46) sts.

Shape Neck and Raglan

Increase Row 1 (Neck and Raglan) (RS): Working back and forth, begin St st. [K1-f/b, slip marker (sm), k1-f/b, work to 1 st before next marker] 3 times, k1-f/b, sm, k1-f/b—40 (42, 44, 46, 48, 50, 54) sts [2 sts each Front; 6 (6, 6, 6, 7, 7, 7) sts each Sleeve; 24 (26, 28, 30, 30, 32, 36) sts for Back]. Work even for 1 row.

Increase Row 2 (Raglan) (RS): [Work to 1 st before first marker, k1-f/b, sm, k1-f/b] 4 times, work to end—48 (50, 52, 54, 56, 58, 62) sts [3 sts each Front; 8 (8, 8, 8, 9, 9, 9) sts each Sleeve; 26 (28, 30, 32, 32, 34, 38) sts for Back]. Work even for 1 row.

Increase Row 3 (Neck and Raglan) (RS): K1-f/b, [work to 1 st before next marker, k1-f/b, sm, k1-f/b] 4 times, work to last st, k1-f/b—58 (60, 62, 64, 66, 68, 72) sts [5 sts each Front; 10 (10, 10, 10, 11, 11, 11) sts each Sleeve; 28 (30, 32, 34, 34, 36, 40) sts for Back].

Repeat last 4 rows 8 (9, 10, 11, 11, 12, 14) times—202 (222, 242, 262, 264, 284, 324) sts [29 (32, 35, 38, 38, 41, 47) sts each Front; 42 (46, 50, 54, 55, 59, 67) sts each Sleeve; 60 (66, 72, 78, 78, 84, 96) sts for Back].

Next Row (RS): Repeat Increase Row 2 this row, then every other row 6 (7, 7, 5, 4, 3, 0) times—258 (286, 306, 310, 304, 316, 332) sts [36 (40, 43, 44, 43, 45, 48) sts each Front; 56 (62, 66, 66, 65, 67, 69) sts each Sleeve; 74 (82, 88, 90, 88, 92, 98) sts for Back]. Mark each end of row with removable marker for finishing.

Divide for Body

Next Row (RS): Work to first marker, remove marker, transfer next 56 (62, 66, 66, 65, 67, 69) sts to waste yarn for Left Sleeve, CO 1 (1, 2, 5, 11, 13, 14) sts for underarm, pm color A for side, CO 1 (1, 2, 5, 11, 13, 14) sts for underarm, remove marker, work to next marker, remove marker, transfer 56 (62, 66, 66, 65, 67, 69) sts to waste yarn for Right Sleeve, CO 1 (1, 2, 5, 11, 13, 14) sts for underarm, pm color A, CO 1 (1, 2, 5, 11, 13, 14) sts for underarm, remove marker, work to end—150 (166, 182, 198, 218, 234, 250) sts remain. Work even for 1 row.

Shape Waist

Set-Up Row (RS): Work 19 (21, 23, 25, 29, 31, 33) sts, pm color B, work to 18 (20, 22, 24, 25, 27, 29) sts after next color A marker, pm color B, work 40 (44, 48, 52, 60, 64, 68) sts, pm color B, work to 18 (20, 22, 24, 25, 27, 29) sts after next color A marker, pm color B, work to end. Work even for 1 row.

Decrease Row (RS): Decrease 4 sts this row, then every 6 rows twice, as follows: [Work to next color B marker, sm, ssk, work to 2 sts before next color B marker, sm, k2tog], work to end—138 (154, 170, 186, 206, 222, 238) sts remain. Work even until piece measures 15 (15½, 16, 16½, 17, 17½, 17½)″ from the beginning, ending with a WS row.

Increase Row (RS): Increase 4 sts this row, then every 6 rows twice, as follows: *Work to next color B marker, sm, m1, work to next color B marker, m1, sm; repeat from * once, work to end—150 (166, 182, 198, 218, 234, 250) sts. Work even until piece measures 21 (21½, 21¾, 22, 23, 23½, 23½)″ from the beginning (removing all markers on first row), ending with a RS row. Work even for 1 row.

Next Row (RS): Change to 2×2 Rib. Work even for 2″. BO all sts in pattern.

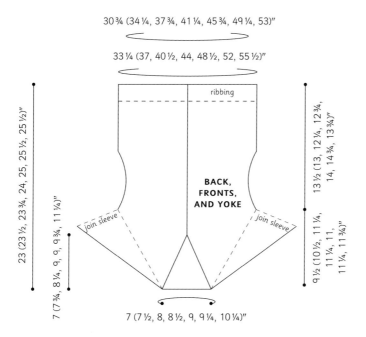

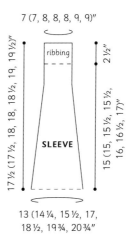

30 ¾ (34 ¼, 37 ¾, 41 ¼, 45 ¾, 49 ¼, 53)"

33 ¼ (37, 40 ½, 44, 48 ½, 52, 55 ½)"

ribbing

7 (7, 8, 8, 8, 9, 9)"

ribbing

2 ½"

23 (23 ½, 23 ¾, 24, 25, 25 ½, 25 ½)"

13 ½ (13, 12 ¼, 12 ¾, 14, 14 ¾, 13 ¾)"

17 ½ (17 ½, 18, 18, 18 ½, 19, 19 ½)"

15 (15, 15 ½, 15 ½, 16, 16 ½, 17)"

SLEEVE

BACK, FRONTS, AND YOKE

join sleeve   join sleeve

7 (7 ¾, 8 ¼, 9, 9, 9 ¾, 11 ¼)"

9 ½ (10 ½, 11 ¼, 11 ¼, 11, 11 ¼, 11 ¾)"

13 (14 ¼, 15 ½, 17, 18 ½, 19 ¾, 20 ¾)"

7 (7 ½, 8, 8 ½, 9, 9 ¼, 10 ¼)"

SLEEVES

Note: Use your preferred method of working in the rnd when working the Sleeves (see page 150).

Transfer Sleeve sts from waste yarn to needle(s). With RS facing, rejoin yarn at underarm; knit to end, pick up and knit 1 (1, 2, 5, 9, 11, 12) sts from sts CO for underarm, pm for beginning of rnd, pick up and knit 1 (1, 2, 5, 9, 11, 12) sts from sts CO for underam, work to end of rnd—58 (64, 70, 76, 83, 89, 93) sts. Work even for 3 rnds.

Shape Sleeve: Decrease 2 sts this rnd, every 5 rnds 11 (10, 9, 0, 0, 0, 0) times, every 4 rnds 0 (4, 6, 16, 7, 7, 3) times, then every 3 rnds 0 (0, 0, 2, 15, 16, 22) times, as follows: K1, k2tog, work to last 3 sts, ssk, k1—34 (34, 38, 38, 37, 41, 41) sts remain. Work even until Sleeve measures 15 (15, 15 ½, 15 ½, 16, 16 ½, 17)" from underarm. Work even for 1 rnd.

Next Rnd: Decrease 2 (2, 2, 2, 1, 1, 1) sts evenly spaced around—32 (32, 36, 36, 36, 40, 40) sts remain.

Next Rnd: Change to 2×2 Rib in-the-Round. Work even for 2 ½". BO all sts in pattern. *Note: The Sleeve is designed to be long, so that you can turn up the cuff.*

COLLAR

With RS facing and beginning at lower corner of Right Front, pick up and knit 3 sts for every 4 rows along Right Front edge to removable marker, pm, remove Front marker, pick up and knit 1 st for each row along right neck edge, 1 st for each CO st along top of shoulders and Back neck, 1 st for each row along left neck edge to removable marker, pm, remove Front marker, and 3 sts for every 4 rows along Left Front edge, making sure that you have a multiple of 4 sts + 2 left over. *Note: If you don't have enough sts to reach the correct multiple, you may increase the additional sts needed on the next row.*

Next Row (WS): P2, *k2, p2; repeat from * to end.

Note: Collar will be shaped using Short Rows (see Special Techniques, page 162). Hide wraps as you come to them.

Shape Collar

Row 1 (RS): Work to 4 sts after last marker, wrp-t.

Row 2: Repeat Row 1.

Rows 3-12: Work to 3 sts after wrapped st of row before last row worked, wrp-t.

Sizes Large, 1X-Large, 2X-Large, and 3X-Large Only

Repeat Row 3 four (four, four, six) times.

All Sizes

Work across all sts, hiding remaining wrap on first row. Work even until Collar measures 3″ from pick-up row, measured at lower Front edge.

SELF-TIE BELT

CO 12 sts.

Row 1 (WS): Slip 1 purlwise, p1, k2, [p2, k2] twice.

Row 2: Slip 1, knit the knit sts and purl the purl sts as they face you.

Repeat Row 2 until piece measures 60 (62, 64, 70, 74, 78, 82)″ or to desired length from the beginning. BO all sts in pattern.

BELT LOOPS (optional)

Try on the Jacket. Tie Belt around waist, and use removable marker to mark location of lower edge of Belt at side of Jacket. Measure length from lower edge of Jacket to marker; record this measurement. Decide on locations of 4 Belt Loops around Jacket, 1 on each Front and 2 on Back. Consider placing Belt Loops either just to one side of or centered over the waist shaping. At each of these locations, measure from the lower edge of Jacket and mark point where bottom of Belt Loop will be.

Using dpn, pick up and knit 4 sts at marker.

Row 1 (WS): K1, p2, k1.

Row 2: P1, k2, p1.

Repeat Rows 1 an 2 until Belt Loop is slightly shorter than width of Self-Tie Belt (Belt will roll and stretch slightly). BO all sts in pattern. Sew BO edge to Jacket.

FINISHING

Block as desired.

MAKE IT YOUR OWN

To dress up this sweater you can cinch the waist with a store-bought belt instead of the knitted one—just be sure to knit your belt loops slightly longer than the width of the belt.

If you want a cardigan with a V-neck instead of a shawl collar, follow the directions under Collar, but pick up an odd number of stitches. Then work knit 1, purl 1 rib for 1½ to 2".

If you want buttonholes, mark their placement on the right-hand side of the garment, and work a couple rows of ribbing. *Note: Work enough rows so that your first buttonhole row will fall roughly in the middle of your band. For instance, if you plan on working 11 rows for the band, you will want your first buttonhole row to fall on Row 6.* Then work a simple two-row buttonhole as follows: On the first row of the buttonhole, work to the placement of the buttonhole. Bind off 2 or more stitches. (Check your button size before deciding the number of stitches that should be bound off. It is better to bind off fewer stitches than more—you don't want a saggy buttonhole!). Continue working in pattern, repeating the bind-off at the next buttonhole placement. On the next row, work to the bound-off stitches, cast on the same number of stitches that you bound off on the previous row. On the following row, work the cast-on stitches through the back loops to tighten them up. When the band is complete, sew your buttons onto the left-hand band. *Note: You will need to reverse this if you are working a man's cardigan. In other words, the buttonholes will be on the left-hand band of the garment, and the buttons will be on the right-hand band.*

SIZES

X-Small (Small, Medium, Large,
1X-Large, 2X-Large, 3X-Large)

FINISHED MEASUREMENTS

32½ (36½, 40½, 43½, 48½,
52½, 56½)" chest

YARN

Karabella Margrite (80%
extrafine merino wool / 20%
cashmere; 154 yards / 50 grams):
5 (6, 6, 7, 8, 8, 9) balls #9290

NEEDLES

One 29" (74 cm) long or longer
circular (circ) needle size US 6
(4 mm)

One 29" (74 cm) long or longer
circ needle size US 4 (3.5 mm)

One or two 24" (60 cm) long or
longer circ needles or one set of
five double-pointed needles (dpn)
size US 6 (4 mm), as preferred,
for Sleeves

One or two 24" (60 cm) long or
longer circ needles or one set of
five dpn size US 4 (3.5 mm), as
preferred, for Sleeves

Change needle size if necessary
to obtain correct gauge.

NOTIONS

Cable needle (cn); stitch markers
in 2 colors; waste yarn

GAUGE

20 sts and 28 rows = 4" (10 cm)
in Stockinette stitch (St st) using
larger needles

BACKWARD CABLED PULLOVER

I can't tell you how many times I've jaunted off to the office feeling sensational only to discover, six hours later while reapplying my lipstick in the fourth-floor washroom, that I am wearing my shirt inside-out and backwards.

Honestly and truly, this sort of thing has happened to me more often than I'd like to report, so I thought I would design a garment that can be worn forward or backward. I confess I considered designing it so it could go inside-out, too, but I'm not that clever. The "back" is worked as a sexy scoop, while short-row shaping in the "front" makes the neckline rise just a bit, giving it a retro feel. If you don't want such a high neckline, or if you're a beginner and you'd rather not dabble in short rows, just omit the shaping. Wear it whichever way you want, depending on mood (or chance). Needless to say, if you're working the main version here and you reverse it by wearing the scoop in the front, you'll want a pretty camisole to wear underneath.

PATTERN FEATURES
Top-down raglan construction, body and sleeves worked in the round, short-row shaping (optional), cables

ABBREVIATIONS

FC (Front Cross): Slip next 3 sts to cn, hold to front, k2, slip last st on cn back to left-hand needle, p1, k2 from cn.

BC (Back Cross): Slip next 3 sts to cn, hold to back, k2, slip last st on cn back to left-hand needle, p1, k2 from cn.

RT (Right Twist): K2tog, but do not drop sts from left-hand needle, insert right-hand needle between 2 sts just worked and knit first st again, slip both sts from left-hand needle together.

STITCH PATTERNS

Cable Panel
(panel of 22 sts; 8-row/rnd repeat)

Rows/Rnds 1 and 5 (RS): P1, k1, p2, [k2, p1] 4 times, k2, p2, k1, p1.

Rows/Rnds 2, 4, and 6: Knit the knit sts and purl the purl sts as they face you.

Row/Rnd 3: P1, k1, p2, k2, [p1, FC] twice, p2, k1, p1.

Row/Rnd 7: P1, k1, p2, [BC, p1] twice, k2, p2, k1, p1.

Row/Rnd 8: Repeat Row/Rnd 2.

Repeat Rows/Rnds 1-8 for Cable Panel.

Baby Cable Rib
(multiple of 4 sts; 4-rnd repeat)
Rnds 1-3: *K2, p2; repeat from * around.
Rnd 4: *RT, p2; repeat from * around.

YOKE

Note: Use stitch markers in 2 colors; 4 in color A for raglan shaping and 2 in color B to mark the Cable Panel.

With larger 29″ long circ needle, CO 2 sts for Back, place marker (pm) color A, 4 (4, 6, 6, 6, 6, 6) sts for Left Sleeve, pm color A, 6 (8, 9, 11, 12, 13, 13) sts for left side of Front, pm color B for beginning of Cable Panel, 22 sts for Cable Panel, pm color B for end of Cable Panel, 6 (8, 9, 11, 12, 13, 13) sts for right side of Front, pm color A, 4 (4, 6, 6, 6, 6, 6) sts for Right Sleeve, pm color A, 2 sts for Back—46 (50, 56, 60, 62, 64, 64) sts.

Shape Raglan

Increase Row 1 (RS): *Knit to 1 st before next color A marker, k1-f/b, slip marker (sm), k1-f/b, knit to 1 st before next color A marker, k1-f/b, sm, k1-f/b*, knit to next color B marker, sm, work Cable Panel across 22 sts, sm, repeat from * to *, knit to end—54 (58, 64, 68, 70, 72, 72) sts.

Begin Short-Row Neck Shaping (optional—see Special Techniques, page 162) *Note: Hide wraps as you come to them.*

Row 1 (WS): Work to 2 (3, 4, 5, 6, 7, 7) sts after second color B marker, wrp-t.

Row 2: Repeat Row 1.

Rows 3 and 4: Work to 3 sts after wrapped st of row before last row worked, wrp-t. Work even for 1 row, hiding last wrap worked.

Next Row (RS): Repeat Increase Row this row, then every other row 5 times—102 (106, 112, 116, 118, 120, 120) sts [48 (52, 54, 58, 60, 62, 62) sts for Front; 18 (18, 20, 20, 20, 20, 20) sts each Sleeve; 9 sts each side of Back]. Work even for 1 row.

Shape Raglan and Neck

Increase Row 2 (RS): K1-f/b, [work to 1 st before next color A marker, k1-f/b, sm, k1-f/b] 4 times, work to last st, k1-f/b—112 (116, 122, 126, 128, 130, 130) sts. Work even for 1 row.

Next Row (RS): Repeat Increase Row 1—120 (124, 130, 134, 136, 138, 138) sts. Work even for 1 row.

Repeat last 4 rows 4 (6, 6, 6, 8, 8, 8) times, then Repeat Increase Row 1 every other row 6 (4, 6, 7, 4, 7, 9) times—240 (264, 286, 298, 312, 338, 354) sts [80 (88, 94, 100, 104, 112, 116) sts for Front; 50 (54, 60, 62, 64, 70, 74) sts each Sleeve; 30 (34, 36, 37, 40, 43, 45) sts each side for Back]. Work even for 1 row.

BODY

Next Row (RS): Work to first color A marker, transfer next 50 (54, 60, 62, 64, 70, 74) sts to waste yarn for Left Sleeve, removing markers, CO 0 (1, 3, 5, 8, 9, 12) sts for underarm, pm for beginning of rnd, CO 0 (1, 3, 5, 8, 9, 12) sts for underarm, work to next color A marker, transfer next 50 (54, 60, 62, 64, 70, 74) sts to waste

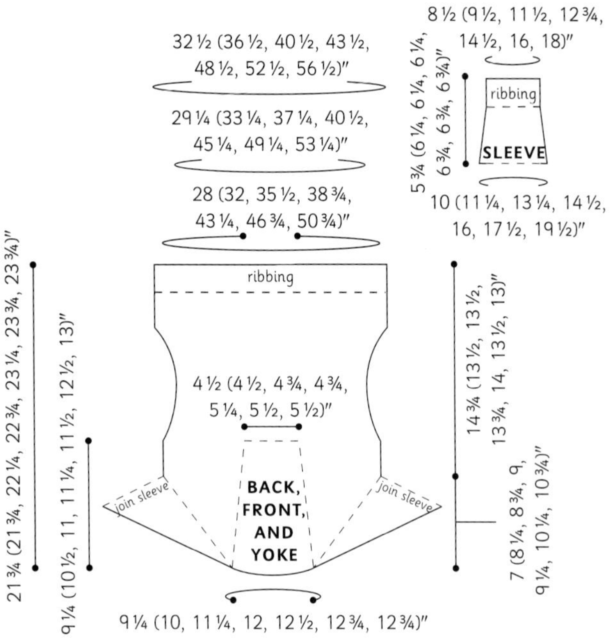
8 ½ (9 ½, 11 ½, 12 ¾, 14 ½, 16, 18)"
32 ½ (36 ½, 40 ½, 43 ½, 48 ½, 52 ½, 56 ½)"
29 ¼ (33 ¼, 37 ¼, 40 ½, 45 ¼, 49 ¼, 53 ¼)"
28 (32, 35 ½, 38 ¾, 43 ¼, 46 ¾, 50 ¾)"
5 ¾ (6 ¼, 6 ¼, 6 ¼, 6 ¾, 6 ¾, 6 ¾)"
ribbing
SLEEVE
10 (11 ¼, 13 ¼, 14 ½, 16, 17 ½, 19 ½)"
ribbing
21 ¾ (21 ¾, 22 ¼, 22 ¾, 23 ¼, 23 ¾, 23 ¾)"
9 ¼ (10 ½, 11, 11 ¼, 11 ½, 12 ½, 13)"
4 ½ (4 ½, 4 ¾, 4 ¾, 5 ¼, 5 ½, 5 ½)"
join sleeve
BACK, FRONT, AND YOKE
join sleeve
14 ¾ (13 ½, 13 ½, 13 ½, 13 ¾, 14, 13 ½, 13)"
7 (8 ¼, 8 ¾, 9, 9 ¼, 10 ¼, 10 ¾)"
9 ¼ (10, 11 ¼, 12, 12 ½, 12 ¾, 12 ¾)"

yarn for Right Sleeve, removing markers, CO 0 (1, 3, 5, 8, 9, 12) sts for underarm, pm, CO 0 (1, 3, 5, 8, 9, 12) sts for underarm, work to end–140 (160, 178, 194, 216, 234, 254) sts.

Shape Back Neck: Work even for 14 rows, CO 22 (22, 24, 24, 26, 28, 28) sts at end of last row using Backward Loop CO Method (see Special Techniques, page 162)–162 (182, 202, 218, 242, 262, 282) sts. *Note: If you prefer a less dramatic Back, work only 2 rows, not 14, before casting on sts for Back neck.* Join for working in the rnd; work to beginning of rnd marker. Work even for 1 rnd. *Note: If you chose to omit 12 rows worked before shaping the Back neck, work them now before shaping the waist.*

Shape Waist

Decrease Rnd: Decrease 4 sts this rnd, then every 7 rnds 3 times, as follows: K1, k2tog, work to 3 sts before next color A marker, ssk, k2, k2tog, work to last 3 sts, ssk, k1–146 (166, 186, 202, 226, 246, 266) sts remain. Work even for 12 rnds.

Increase Rnd: Increase 4 sts this rnd, then every 7 rnds 3 times, as follows: K1, m1, work to 1 st before next color A marker, m1, k2, m1, work to last st, m1, k1–164 (184, 204, 220, 244, 264, 284) sts. Work even until piece measures 20 (20, 20 ½, 21, 21 ½, 22, 22)" from the beginning, increase 2 sts evenly spaced on last rnd–162 (182, 202, 222, 242, 262, 282) sts.

Next Rnd: Change to smaller circ needle and Baby Cable Rib. Work even for 12 rnds. BO all sts loosely in pattern.

SLEEVES

Note: Use your preferred method of working in the rnd when working the Sleeves (see page 150).

Transfer Sleeve sts from waste yarn to larger needle(s). With RS facing, join yarn at underarm, work to end, pick up and knit 0 (1, 3, 5, 8, 9, 12) sts from sts CO for underarm, pm for beginning of rnd, pick up and knit 0 (1, 3, 5, 8, 9, 12) sts from sts CO for underarm–50 (56, 66, 72, 80, 88, 98) sts. Join for working in the rnd. Work to beginning of rnd. Work even for 3 rnds.

Shape Sleeve: Decrease 2 sts this rnd, then every 7 rnds 3 times, as follows: K1, k2tog, work to last 3 sts, ssk, k1–42 (48, 58, 64, 72, 80, 90) sts remain. Work even until Sleeve measures 4 (4 ½, 4 ½, 4 ½, 5, 5, 5)" from underarm, decrease 2 (0, 2, 0, 0, 0, 2) sts evenly spaced on last rnd–40 (48, 56, 64, 72, 80, 88) sts remain.

Next Rnd: Change to smaller needle(s) and Baby Cable Rib. Work even for 12 rnds. BO all sts loosely in pattern.

FINISHING

Neckband: With RS facing, using smaller 29" circ needle, beginning at right Back shoulder, pick up and knit approximately 2 sts for every 3 rows along right Back neck edge, 1 st for every CO st across center Back, 2 sts for every 3 rows along left Back neck edge, 1 st for every CO st along Left Sleeve top, 1 st for every CO st across Front neck, and 1 st for every CO st across Right Sleeve top, making sure you have a multiple of 4 sts. Join for working in the rnd; pm for beginning of rnd. Begin Baby Cable Rib. Work even for 12 rnds. BO all sts loosely in pattern. *Note: When binding off center Back sts, you may want to work 2 sts together in each corner so the ribbing lays flat.*

Close up any holes at underarms, if necessary. Block as desired.

MAKE IT YOUR OWN

The variation shown here has capped sleeves, and the scoop neck and cables face forward. To make this variation, move the 22 cable stitches from the Front to the Back by placing the 2 cable markers on the Back center 22 stitches instead of the Front center 22 stitches.

To raise the neckline like the variation shown here, refer to the pattern in the Shape Back Neck section for instructions.

For cap sleeves, transfer the Sleeve stitches to one or more circular or double-pointed needles, as preferred, and join for working in the round, as instructed in the pattern. After working one plain knit round, work one set of paired decreases at the center underarm (example: k1, k2tog, work to 3 sts before marker, ssk, k1) and then a round of plain knitting. Count your stitches, and make sure you have a multiple of 4 for the upcoming rib pattern. If not, work an additional set of decreases on your next round. Change to smaller needles and work the Baby Cable Rib as instructed in the pattern. Bind off all stitches loosely in pattern.

The variation was worked in a size X-Small with 5 balls of the same yarn as the main version, but in color #18. Read about estimating yarn requirements on page 160.

INGENUE

What can I say? I'm a sucker for anything that has a retro—but timeless—aesthetic, and if it's sprinkled with a bit of Audrey Hepburn or maybe Leslie Caron (that gal who played Gigi), in two seconds flat I'll be shaking like a Chihuahua with too many tall people in the room.

   This wide-neck pullover is a relatively quick knit. It's constructed so you start the neckband first and the rest of the sweater literally grows out from it, meaning you'll have just one tiny bit of finishing to do. The three-quarter sleeves are slightly belled, and they feature the same stitch pattern as the neckline. This pattern is perfect for a beginner because it's basic with just a little bit of special stitching that looks more complex than it really is.

PATTERN FEATURES
Top-down raglan construction, body and sleeves worked in the round, short-repeat stitch pattern

---

SIZES
X-Small (Small, Medium, Large, 1X-Large, 2X-Large, 3X-Large)

FINISHED MEASUREMENTS
30¼ (33, 37¼, 41, 45¼, 49¾, 51½)" chest

YARN
Karabella Marble (55% wool / 45% alpaca superfine; 95 yards / 50 grams): 9 (9, 10, 11, 12, 13, 14) balls #35354

NEEDLES
One 29" (74 cm) long or longer circular (circ) needle size US 8 (5 mm)

One 24" (60 cm) long circ needle size US 8 (5 mm) (sizes X-Small and Small only)

One or two 24" (60 cm) long or longer circ needles or one set of five double-pointed needles (dpn) size US 8 (5 mm), as preferred, for Sleeves

Change needle size if necessary to obtain correct gauge.

NOTIONS
Stitch markers in 3 colors; waste yarn

GAUGE
18 sts and 22 rows = 4" (10 cm) in Stockinette stitch (St st)

STITCH PATTERN

Ridge Stitch
(multiple of 2 sts; 4-rnd repeat)
Rnd 1: Knit.
Rnd 2: *P2tog; repeat from * to end.
Rnd 3: *K1-f/b; repeat from * to end.
Rnd 4: Knit.
Repeat Rnds 1-4 for Ridge Stitch.

NECKBAND

Note: Change to longer circ needle if necessary for number of sts on needle.

With 29″ long circ needle (sizes X-Small and Small, use 24″ long circ needle), CO 116 (120, 124, 128, 132, 136, 140) sts. Join for working in the rnd, being careful not to twist sts; place marker (pm) color A for beginning of rnd. Begin Ridge Stitch. Work even until 10 vertical repeats of pattern have been completed.

YOKE
Shape Raglan

Set-Up Rnd: Change to St st (knit every rnd). K24 for Left Sleeve, pm color B, k34 (36, 38, 40, 42, 44, 46) for Front, pm color B, k24 for Right Sleeve, pm color B, knit across Back to end.

Increase Rnd: Increase 8 sts this rnd, then every other rnd 16 (17, 18, 20, 21, 22, 24) times, as follows: K1, m1, [work to 1 st before next color B marker, m1, k1, slip marker (sm), k1, m1] 3 times, work to last st, m1, k1—252 (264, 276, 296, 308, 320, 340) sts [58 (60, 62, 66, 68, 70, 74) sts each Sleeve; 68 (72, 76, 82, 86, 90, 96) sts each for Front and Back].

BODY

Join Back and Front: Transfer next 58 (60, 62, 66, 68, 70, 74) sts to waste yarn for Left Sleeve, removing markers, CO 0 (1, 4, 5, 8, 11, 10) sts for underarm, reposition color A marker for new beginning of rnd, CO 0 (1, 4, 5, 8, 11, 10) sts for underarm, work to next marker, transfer next 58 (60, 62, 66, 68, 70, 74) sts to waste yarn for Left Sleeve, removing markers, CO 0 (1, 4, 5, 8, 11, 10) sts for underarm, place color C marker for side, CO 0 (1, 4, 5, 8, 11, 10) sts for underarm, work to end—136 (148, 168, 184, 204, 224, 232) sts remain. *Note: Size X-Small will just place marker between Front and Back without casting on any sts for the underarm.* Continuing in St st, work even for 10 rnds.

Shape Waist

Note: Change to shorter circ needle if necessary for number of sts remaining. Waist decreases will occur within the Front and Back, rather than at the sides; waist increases will occur at the sides.

Set-Up Rnd: Work 18 (18, 22, 24, 26, 28, 30) sts, pm color B, work 32 (38, 40, 44, 50, 56, 56) sts, pm color B, work to next marker, sm, work 18 (18, 22, 24, 26, 28, 30) sts, pm color B, work 32 (38, 40, 44, 50, 56, 56) sts, pm color B, work to end.

Decrease Rnd: Decrease 4 sts this rnd, then every 5 rnds 3 times, as follows: Work to 2 sts before first color B marker, ssk, sm, work to next color B marker, sm, k2tog, work to 2 sts before next color B marker, slipping color C marker as you come to it, ssk, work to next color B marker, sm, k2tog, work to end—120 (132, 152, 168, 188, 208, 216) sts remain. Work even for 5 rnds, removing color B markers on first rnd.

Increase Rnd: Increase 4 sts this rnd, then every 5 rnds 3 times, as follows: K1, m1, work to 1 st before next marker, m1, k1, sm, k1, m1, work to last st, m1, k1—136 (148, 168, 184, 204, 224, 232) sts. Work even for 5 rnds.

Next Rnd: Change to Ridge Stitch. Work even until 4 vertical repeats of pattern have been completed. Knit 1 rnd. Purl 1 rnd. BO all sts loosely knitwise.

SLEEVES

Note: Use your preferred method of working in the rnd when working the Sleeves (see page 150).

Transfer Sleeve sts to needle(s). With RS facing, rejoin yarn at armhole; knit to end, pick up and knit 0 (2, 8, 10, 12, 18, 16) sts from sts CO for underarm—58 (62, 70, 76, 80, 88, 90) sts. *Note: You will not pick up from every CO st for the 3 largest sizes.* Join for working in the rnd. Work even for 4 rnds.

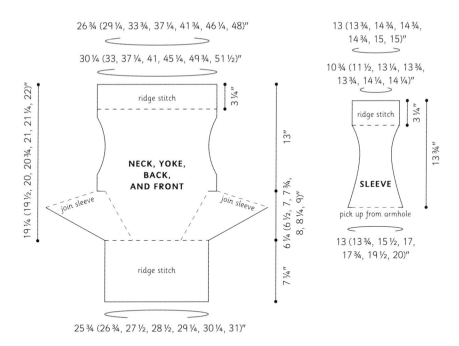

26 ¾ (29 ¼, 33 ¾, 37 ¼, 41 ¾, 46 ¼, 48)"

30 ¼ (33, 37 ¼, 41, 45 ¼, 49 ¾, 51 ½)"

13 (13 ¾, 14 ¾, 14 ¾, 14 ¾, 15, 15)"

10 ¾ (11 ½, 13 ¼, 13 ¾, 13 ¾, 14 ¼, 14 ¼)"

ridge stitch

3 ¼"

ridge stitch

3 ¼"

13"

13 ¾"

NECK, YOKE, BACK, AND FRONT

SLEEVE

19 ¼ (19 ½, 20, 20 ¾, 21, 21 ¼, 22)"

join sleeve

join sleeve

pick up from armhole

6 ¼ (6 ½, 7, 7 ¾, 8, 8 ¼, 9)"

ridge stitch

7 ¼"

13 (13 ¾, 15 ½, 17, 17 ¾, 19 ½, 20)"

25 ¾ (26 ¾, 27 ½, 28 ½, 29 ¼, 30 ¼, 31)"

Shape Sleeve

Decrease Rnd: Decrease 2 sts this rnd, then every 5 (5, 6, 5, 4, 2, 2) rnds 4 (4, 4, 6, 8, 11, 12) times, as follows: K1, k2tog, work to last 3 sts, ssk, k1–48 (52, 60, 62, 62, 64, 64) sts remain. Work even for 10 rnds.

Increase Rnd: Increase 2 sts this rnd, then every 5 (5, 8, 9, 7, 18, 18) rnds 4 (4, 2, 1, 1, 1, 1) times, as follows: K1, m1, work to last st, m1, k1–58 (62, 66, 66, 66, 68, 68) sts. Work even for 1 rnd.

Next Rnd: Change to Ridge Stitch. Work even until 4 vertical repeats of pattern have been completed. Knit 1 rnd. Purl 1 rnd. BO all sts loosely knitwise.

FINISHING

Fold neck in half to WS and sew to top of Yoke, being careful not to let sts show on RS. Block as desired.

MAKE IT YOUR OWN

You could easily make this an off-the-shoulder sweater: When working the Neckband, instead of using the stitch pattern as directed, change to a stretchy knit 2, purl 2 rib and work until the desired Neckband depth is reached. Then, change to Stockinette stitch and work the pattern as directed. Add 2×2 rib at the cuffs and bottom edge to match the Neckband.

LION-NECK CARDIGAN

I would call this a "Make the Most of What You Have or Don't Have" garment because it is oddly slenderizing, yet adds some curves, too. Normally, I wouldn't use such a chunky yarn because, let's face it, chunky is what chunky does. But if you're careful to select a lofty yet drapey yarn, you're likely to end up with a flattering garment that skims over your body rather than one that adds bulk, turning you into some sort of girly linebacker.

This cardigan is worked in one piece from the top down, with a ruffle at the fronts and collar. Note that the fronts are meant to be open slightly, so don't panic if you count the front stitches and discover there are fewer than there are on the back.

PATTERN FEATURES
Top-down raglan construction, sleeves worked in the round, single crochet

---

SIZES

X-Small (Small, Medium, Large, 1X-Large, 2X-Large, 3X-Large)

FINISHED MEASUREMENTS

23¼ (26, 27¼, 32, 36¾, 41¼, 44¾)" chest

Note: Cardigan will lay open slightly in the front.

YARN

Rowan Yarns Classic Soft Tweed (56% wool / 20% viscose / 14% polyamide / 10% silk; 87 yards / 50 grams): 8 (8, 9, 10, 12, 13, 14) balls #8 blanket

NEEDLES

One 29" (74 cm) long or longer circular (circ) needle size US 11 (8 mm)

One 16" (40 cm) long circ needle size US 11 (8 mm)

One or two 24" (60 cm) long or longer circ needles or one set of five double-pointed needles (dpn) size US 11 (8 mm), as preferred, for Sleeves

One 40" (100 cm) long or longer circ needle size US 11 (8 mm), for neckband

Change needle size if necessary to obtain correct gauge.

NOTIONS

Crochet hook size US L-11 (8mm); stitch markers; waste yarn

GAUGE

12 sts and 16 rows = 4" (10 cm) in Stockinette stitch (St st)

STITCH PATTERNS

3×1 Rib
(multiple of 4 sts + 3; 1-row repeat)
Row 1 (RS): *K3, p1; repeat from * to last 3 sts, k3.
Row 2: Knit the knit sts and purl the purl sts as they face you.
Repeat Row 2 for 3×1 Rib.

3×1 Rib in-the-Round
(multiple of 4 sts; 1-rnd repeat)
All Rnds: *K3, p1; repeat from * around.

1×1 Rib
(multiple of 2 sts + 1; 1-row repeat)
Row 1 (WS): *P1, k1; repeat from * to last st, p1.
Row 2: Knit the knit sts and purl the purl sts as they face you.
Repeat Row 2 for 1×1 Rib.

NOTE
The front measurement is slightly narrower than the back, allowing the cardigan to lay open slightly.

YOKE
With 29″ long circ needle, CO 1 st for Right Front, place marker (pm), 1 (2, 2, 2, 4, 4, 4) sts for Right Sleeve, pm, 12 (12, 12, 14, 16, 18, 20) sts for Back, pm, 1 (2, 2, 2, 4, 4, 4) sts for Left Sleeve, pm, and 1 st for Left Front—16 (18, 18, 20, 26, 28, 30) sts.

Shape Raglan

Increase Row 1 (RS): Begin St st. [K1-f/b, slip marker (sm), k1-f/b, work to 1 st before next marker] 3 times, k1-f/b, sm, k1-f/b—24 (26, 26, 28, 34, 36, 38) sts. Purl 1 row.

Increase Row 2 (RS): [Work to 1 st before marker, k1-f/b, sm, k1-f/b] 4 times, work to end—32 (34, 36, 42, 42, 44, 46) sts. Purl 1 row.

Repeat last 2 rows 11 (13, 14, 16, 19, 20, 20) times—120 (138 146, 164, 194, 204, 206) sts [14 (16, 17, 19, 22, 23, 23) sts each Front; 27 (32, 34, 38, 46, 48, 48) sts each Sleeve; 38 (42, 44, 50, 58, 62, 64) sts for Back].

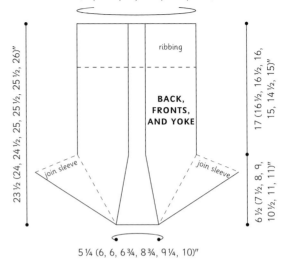

23 ¼ (26, 27 ¼, 32, 36 ¾, 41 ¼, 44 ¾)″

ribbing

BACK, FRONTS, AND YOKE

join sleeve   join sleeve

23 ½ (24, 24 ½, 25, 25 ½, 25 ½, 26)″

17 (16 ½, 16 ½, 16, 15, 14 ½, 15)″

6 ½ (7 ½, 8, 9, 10 ½, 11, 11)″

5 ¼ (6, 6, 6 ¾, 8 ¾, 9 ¼, 10)″

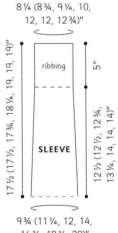

8 ¼ (8 ¾, 9 ¼, 10, 12, 12, 12 ¾)″

ribbing

SLEEVE

5″

17 ½ (17 ½, 17 ¾, 18 ¼, 19, 19, 19)″

12 ½ (12 ½, 12 ¾, 13 ¼, 14, 14, 14)″

9 ¾ (11 ¼, 12, 14, 16 ¾, 18 ¾, 20)″

BODY

Work to second marker, remove marker, place next 27 (32, 34, 38, 46, 48, 48) sts on waste yarn for Right Sleeve, remove marker, CO 2 (2, 2, 4, 4, 8, 12) sts for underarm, work to next marker, place next 27 (32, 34, 38, 46, 48, 48) sts on waste yarn for Left Sleeve, removing markers, CO 2 (2, 2, 4, 4, 8, 12) sts for underarm, work to end—70 (78, 82, 96, 110, 124, 134) sts remain. Continuing in St st, work even until piece measures 12 (11½, 11½, 11, 10, 9½, 10)" from armhole, ending with a RS row, increase 1 (1, 1, 0, 1, 3, 1) sts evenly across last row—71 (79, 83, 96, 111, 127, 135) sts.

Change to 3×1 Rib; work even for 5", decrease 1 st on first row for Size Large only. BO all sts loosely in pattern.

SLEEVES

Note: Use your preferred method of working in the rnd when working the Sleeves (see page 150).

Transfer Sleeve sts from waste yarn to needle(s). With RS facing, join yarn at underarm; work to end, pick up and knit 1 (1, 1, 2, 2, 4, 6) sts from sts CO for underarm, pm for beginning of rnd, pick up and knit 1 (1, 1, 2, 2, 4, 6) sts from sts CO for underarm—29 (34, 36, 42, 50, 56, 60) sts. Join for working in the rnd. Continuing in St st, work even for 4 rnds.

Shape Sleeve: Decrease 2 sts this rnd, then every 4 rnds 1 (3, 3, 5, 6, 9, 10) times, as follows: K1, k2tog, work to last 3 sts, ssk, k1—25 (26, 26, 30, 36, 36, 38) sts remain. Work even until piece measures 12½ (12½, 12¾, 13¼, 14, 14, 14)" from underarm, increase 3 (2, 0, 2, 0, 0, 2) sts evenly spaced on last rnd—28 (28, 28, 32, 36, 36, 40) sts.

Change to 3×1 Rib in-the-Round; work even for 5". BO all sts loosely in pattern.

FINISHING

Neckband: With RS facing, using 40" long circ needle, pick up and knit approximately 2 sts for every 3 rows along Right Front, 1 st for every CO st along top of Sleeves and Back, and approximately 2 sts for every 3 rows along Left Front, ending with an odd number of sts. Do NOT join. Begin 1×1 Rib. Work even for 5 rows.

Increase Row 1 (RS): *K1, m1, p1; repeat from * to last st, k1. Work even in 2×1 Rib for 3 rows.

Increase Row 2 (RS): *K2, m1, p1; repeat from * to last st, k1. Work even in 3×1 Rib for 3 rows.

BO all sts loosely in pattern. Close up underarm gaps, if necessary.

Try on Cardigan and mark position of Ties, just below bust on each Front. Using crochet hook, work Crochet Chain (see Special Techniques, page 162) approximately 9" long at each marker. Fasten off.

Block as desired.

MAKE IT YOUR OWN

If you have enough yarn (see page 160 to estimate), you can easily transform this cardigan into an opera coat. Just keep working the Body forever and ever until, when you try the thing on, it reaches the length you want minus the ribbed edging (5"). Add your ribbing, and you're off to the opera! Note that you will need extra-long circular needles to accommodate all of the stitches for the ruffle. Or, you could use two or three circular needles in a row.

If you want to skip the ruffle altogether, just pick up the stitches along the Fronts and neckband as instructed and work a no-nonsense ribbing, then add a self-tie belt later. But know this: Without the ruffles you might miss a glamorous opportunity to get coffee one morning and, at exactly the right moment, push the ruffle off your neck "just so" when an old flame approaches you. He'll say, "Oh, hello! I've missed you; where oh where have you been?" And you'll say, while fluffing the ruffled collar and breezing back a stray lock of wavy hair, "Do I know you? Have we met before?"

FINISHED MEASUREMENTS

26 (30¾, 36¾, 40, 44, 50, 53¼)"
chest

YARN

Lorna's Laces Shepherd Sport
(100% superwash wool; 200
yards / 74 grams): 3 (4, 4, 5, 5,
6, 6) hanks #44ns old rose (MC)

Crystal Palace Yarns Kid Merino
(28% kid mohair / 28% merino
wool / 44% micro nylon; 240
yards / 25 grams): 1 ball #4669
blush (A) (optional)

NEEDLES

One 24" (60 cm) long or longer
circular (circ) needle size US 4
(3.5 mm)

One set of five double-pointed
needles (dpn) size US 3 (3.25
mm)

One or two 24" (60 cm) long or
longer circ needles or one set of
five dpn size US 3 (3.25 mm), as
preferred, for Sleeves

Change needle size if necessary
to obtain correct gauge.

NOTIONS

Crochet hook size US E/4 (3.5
mm) (optional); waste yarn;
stitch markers in 2 colors

GAUGE

24 sts and 28 rows = 4" (10 cm)
in Stockinette stitch (St st) using
larger needles

SKINNY EMPIRE

There's a delicate balance between what is fun to knit and what looks good. Some knitters will argue that knitting is their opportunity to show off their skills—and there is some truth in that—but you gotta love plain old Stockinette stitch. As long as your tension stays true and you use decent fibers, most of the time you will be graced with a garment that drapes well and is flattering to your body. This is especially true if you add some shaping here and there and just a few style elements that elevate the garment from sort of plain to truly elegant. In this case, I took a simple top-down raglan structure and added a scoop neck and an empire waist with a nifty I-cord-type edging that is actually worked as you knit the sweater instead of after the fact. The ruffled neckline is added on at the end, and for kicks, I found a bit of kid merino to line the inside of the ruffle, which is optional.

YOKE

With larger 24" long circ needle, CO 2 (2, 2, 4, 6, 8, 8) sts for right side of Front, place marker (pm), 8 (6, 8, 8, 8, 8, 6) sts for Right Sleeve, pm, 30 (34, 38, 42, 46, 50, 54) sts for Back, pm, 8 (6, 8, 8, 8, 8, 6) sts for Left Sleeve, pm, and 2 (2, 2, 4, 6, 8, 8) sts for left side of Front—50 (50, 58, 66, 74, 82, 82) sts.

Shape Raglan (RS): Working back and forth, begin St st, increase 8 sts this row, then every other row 5 (5, 5, 6, 6, 7, 8) times, as follows: [Work to one st before marker, k1-f/b, slip marker (sm), k1-f/b] 4 times, work to end—98 (98, 106, 122, 130, 146, 154) sts [8 (8, 8, 11, 13, 16, 17) sts each side of Front; 20 (18, 20, 22, 22, 24, 24) sts each Sleeve; 42 (46, 50, 56, 60, 66, 72) sts for Back].

> PATTERN FEATURES
> Top-down raglan construction, body and sleeves worked in the round,
> knitting a stitch together with one from another row, single crochet

ABBREVIATIONS

K1B: Insert right-hand needle from bottom to top into purl st on WS, 4 rnds below next st on left-hand needle. Place st on left-hand needle and knit it together with next st on left-hand needle.

STITCH PATTERN

1×1 Rib
(multiple of 2 sts; 1-rnd repeat)
All Rnds: *K1, p1; repeat from * around.

Shape Raglan and Neck (RS): Increase 10 sts this row, then every other row 7 (8, 9, 9, 9, 9, 9) times, as follows: K1-f/b, [work to one st before marker, k1-f/b, sm, k1-f/b] 4 times, work to last st, k1-f/b—178 (188, 206, 222, 230, 246, 254) sts [24 (26, 28, 31, 33, 36, 37) sts each side of Front; 36 (36, 40, 42, 42, 44, 44) sts each Sleeve; 58 (64, 70, 76, 80, 86, 92) sts for Back].

Next Row (RS): [Work to one st before marker, k1-f/b, sm, k1-f/b] 4 times, work to end, using Backward Loop CO (see Special Techniques, page 162), CO 10 (12, 14, 14, 14, 14, 18) sts—196 (208, 228, 244, 252, 268, 280) sts [25 (27, 29, 32, 34, 37, 38) sts for right side of Front; 38 (38, 42, 44, 44, 46, 46) sts each Sleeve; 60 (66, 72, 78, 82, 88, 94) sts for Back; 35 (39, 43, 46, 48, 51, 56) sts for left side of Front].

BODY

Join Yoke: Join for working in the rnd; pm (different color) for beginning of rnd [60 (66, 72, 78, 82, 88, 94) sts for Front]. Continuing in St st (knit every rnd), work even for 1 rnd.

Shape Raglan: Increase 8 sts this rnd, then every other rnd 6 (8, 11, 12, 14, 17, 17) times, as follows: [Work to one st before marker, k1-f/b, sm, k1-f/b] 4 times, work to end of rnd—252 (280, 324, 348, 372, 412, 424) sts [74 (84, 96, 104, 112, 124, 130) sts each for Front and Back; 52 (56, 66, 70, 74, 82, 82) sts each Sleeve].

Next Rnd: Work to first marker, place next 52 (56, 66, 70, 74, 82, 82) sts on waste yarn for Right Sleeve, removing markers, CO 2 (4, 7, 8, 10, 13, 15) sts, pm for

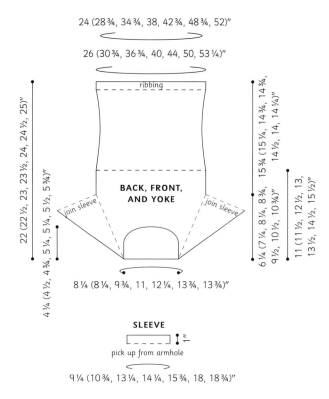

24 (28¾, 34¾, 38, 42¾, 48¾, 52)"

26 (30¾, 36¾, 40, 44, 50, 53¼)"

ribbing

22 (22½, 23, 23½, 24, 24½, 25)"

BACK, FRONT, AND YOKE

join sleeve   *join sleeve*

15¾ (15¼, 14¾, 14¾, 14¾, 14, 14¼)"

14½"

11 (11½, 12½, 13, 13½, 14½, 15½)"

6¼ (7¼, 8¼, 8¾, 9½, 10½, 10¾)"

9½, 10½, 10¾)"

4¼ (4½, 4¾, 5¼, 5½, 5½, 5¾)"

8¼ (8¼, 9¾, 11, 12¼, 13¾, 13¾)"

SLEEVE

pick up from armhole

9¼ (10¾, 13¼, 14¼, 15¾, 18, 18¾)"

beginning of rnd, CO 2 (4, 7, 8, 10, 13, 15) sts, work to next marker, place next 52 (56, 66, 70, 74, 82, 82) sts on waste yarn for Left Sleeve, removing markers, CO 2 (4, 7, 8, 10, 13, 15) sts, pm for side, CO 2 (4, 7, 8, 10, 13, 15) sts—156 (184, 220, 240, 264, 300, 320) sts. Continuing in St st, work even until piece measures 11 (11½, 12½, 13, 13½, 14½, 15½)" from top of shoulder. Work even for 4 rnds.

Establish Empire Waist: *K1B; repeat from * to end of rnd. Work even for 5 rnds.

Shape Waist

Set-Up Rnd: *Work 20 (23, 27, 30, 33, 37, 40) sts, pm color B, work 38 (46, 56, 60, 66, 76, 80) sts, pm color B*, work to side marker, sm; repeat from * to *, work to end of rnd.

Decrease Rnd: [Work to 2 sts before next color B marker, ssk, sm, work to next color B marker, sm, k2tog] twice, work to end of rnd—152 (180, 216, 236, 260, 296, 316) sts remain. Work even for 6 rnds.

Repeat last 7 rnds 2 (2, 2, 2, 1, 1, 1) time(s)–144 (172, 208, 228, 256, 292, 312) sts remain. Work even until piece measures 16 (16 ½, 17, 17 ¼, 17 ½, 17 ¾, 18)" from top of shoulder.

Increase Rnd: [Work to next color B marker, m1, sm, work to next color B marker, sm, m1] twice, work to end of rnd–148 (176, 212, 232, 260, 296, 316) sts. Work even for 6 rnds.

Repeat last 7 rnds 2 (2, 2, 2, 3, 3, 3) times–156 (184, 220, 240, 272, 308, 328) sts. Work even until piece measures 21 (21 ½, 22, 22 ½, 23, 23 ½, 24)" from top of shoulder.

Change to 1×1 Rib; work even for 1". BO all sts loosely in pattern.

SLEEVES

Note: Use your preferred method of working in the rnd for the Sleeves (see page 150). Transfer Sleeve sts from waste yarn to smaller needle(s). With RS facing, join yarn at underarm; work to end, pick up and knit 2 (4, 7, 8, 10, 13, 15) sts from sts CO for underarm, pm for beginning of rnd, pick up and knit 2 (4, 7, 8, 10, 13, 15) sts from sts CO for underarm–56 (64, 80, 86, 94, 108, 112) sts. Join for working in the rnd; pm for beginning of rnd. Knit 1 rnd. Change to 1×1 Rib; work even for 6 rnds. BO all sts loosely in pattern.

FINISHING

Ruffled Neckband: With RS facing, using smaller circ needle, beginning at left Back shoulder, pick up and knit 6 (6, 8, 8, 9, 9, 9) sts across shoulder, 62 (68, 72, 80, 89, 95, 101) sts around Front neck shaping, 6 (6, 8, 8, 9, 9, 9) sts across right shoulder, and 26 (30, 32, 34, 38, 42, 46) sts across Back neck–100 (110, 120, 130, 145, 155, 165) sts. Join for working in the rnd; pm for beginning of rnd.

Rnd 1: *[Knit into front, back, then front of 1 st], k4; repeat from * around–140 (154, 168, 182, 203, 217, 231) sts.

Rnds 2, 4, and 6: Knit.

Rnd 3: *K1, k1-f/b, k4, k1-f/b; repeat from * around–180 (198, 216, 234, 261, 279, 297) sts.

Rnd 5: *K3, k1-f/b, k4, k1-f/b; repeat from * around–220 (242, 264, 286, 319, 341, 363) sts.

BO all sts loosely.

Crochet Edging (optional): With WS facing, using crochet hook and A, work 1 rnd single crochet around pick-up ridge. Fasten off.

Block as desired.

MAKE IT YOUR OWN

Try on as you go and give yourself full-length sleeves by continuing to work them until you get to the desired length, shaping them as you go (see Adjusting Shaping, page 148). Add the ruffles at the edge of your sleeves if you're feeling especially girly. To do this, work Rounds 1-6 of the Ruffled Neckband. Note that you will need to have stitches in a multiple of 5 before you begin Round 1; if you don't, you may adjust the number of stitches that you have on the needle, or you may work more or fewer stitches between increase stitches on Round 1 (keeping in mind that you need to work this same number of stitches between increases on Rounds 3 and 5 as well).

SIZES

Small/Medium (Large, 1X-Large, 2X-Large)

FINISHED MEASUREMENTS

48¾ (57¾, 62½, 67)" at widest point (near elbows), with Front Bands

YARN

Cascade Yarns Ecological Wool (100% natural Peruvian wool; 478 yards / 250 grams): 2 (3, 3, 3) hanks #8049

Note: This yarn comes in very large hanks. If you wish to substitute another yarn, you will need 900 (1025, 1125, 1200) yards.

NEEDLES

One 32" (82 cm) long or longer circular needle (circ) size US 10 (6 mm)

Change needle size if necessary to obtain correct gauge.

NOTIONS

Stitch markers; approximately 3 yards 1½" wide ribbon; seven jumbo snaps; matching sewing thread; sewing needle

GAUGE

14 sts and 16 rows = 4" (10 cm) in Stockinette stitch (St st)

NOT-A-PONCHO CITY CAPE

Okay, I admit it: I am a closet poncho lover. In my mind, you can't beat the ease of just throwing a poncho over the ole head and having your hands free. But after a big poncho craze a few years ago, I have noticed knitters are now on strike, claiming ponchos are tired, out of style, and have been done to death. Even though this cape is basically a poncho, if you're a closet poncho lover like me, you'll be able to knit this up and fool your friends. If they look at you sideways, just remind them that it's a cape—honestly, you'll be sensational in it no matter what.

To give it some pep, I've added a length of vintage ribbon to both sides of what would normally be your button and buttonhole bands, as well as to the arm slits. Instead of buttons, I stitched on some jumbo snaps. You can do the button thing if you want to, but I think that the snaps freshen it up.

> **PATTERN FEATURES**
> *Top-down raglan construction, ribbon and snaps sewn on using a needle and thread*

STITCH PATTERN

2×2 Rib

(multiple of 4 sts + 2; 2-row repeat)
Row 1 (RS): K2, *p2, k2; repeat from * to end.
Row 2: P2, *k2, p2; repeat from * to end.
Repeat Rows 1 and 2 for 2×2 Rib.

YOKE

CO 2 sts for Right Front, place marker (pm), 4 sts for Right Side, pm, 12 (14, 16, 20) sts for Back, pm, 4 sts for Left Side, pm, and 2 sts for Left Front—24 (26, 28, 32) sts. Begin St st, beginning with a WS (purl) row. Work even for 1 row.

Shape Raglan

Increase Row (RS): Working back and forth, increase 8 sts this row, then every other row 5 times, as follows: [Work to one st before next marker, m1, k1, sm, k1, m1] 4 times, work to end—72 (74, 76, 80) sts [8 sts each Front; 16 sts each Side; 24 (26, 28, 32) sts Back]. Work even for 1 row.

Next Row (RS): CO 4 (5, 6, 8) sts, [work to one st before next marker, m1, k1, sm, k1, m1] 4 times, work to end, CO 4 (5, 6, 8) sts—88 (92, 96, 104) sts [13 (14, 15, 17) sts each Front; 18 sts each Side; 26 (28, 30, 34) sts Back]. Work even for 1 row.

Next Row (RS): Repeat Increase Row this row, every other row 9 (13, 15, 20) times, then every 4 rows 4 (3, 2, 0) times—200 (228, 240, 272) sts [27 (31, 33, 38) sts each Front; 46 (52, 54, 60) sts each Side; 54 (62, 66, 76) sts Back]. Work even until piece measures 12 ½ (13 ½, 13 ½, 13 ½)″ from the beginning, ending with a WS row.

Shape Arm Slit Facings (RS): Work to first marker, remove marker, CO 9 sts for facing, join a second ball of yarn, CO 9 sts for facing, work to last marker, removing all markers, CO 9 sts for facing, join a third ball of yarn, CO 9 sts for facing, work to end—36 (40, 42, 47) sts each Front; 164 (184, 192, 214) sts Back/Sides. Working all 3 pieces at same time, work even until arm slits measure 7 (7 ½, 7 ½, 7 ½)″, ending with a WS row.

Next Row (RS): Work to last 9 sts of Right Front section, BO 9 sts, cut yarn and fasten off. BO 9 sts of Back/Sides section, work to last 9 sts of Back/Sides section, BO 9 sts, cut yarn and fasten off. BO 9 sts of Left Front, work to end—200 (228, 240, 272) sts remain. Working across all sts, work even until piece measures 21 ½ (23, 23, 23)″ from the beginning, ending with a WS row, inc 2 sts across last row—202 (230, 242, 274) sts.

Next Row (RS): Change to 2×2 Rib. Work even for 3 ½″. BO all sts loosely in pattern.

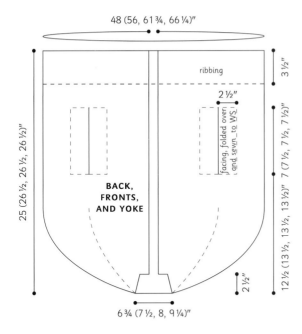

48 (56, 61 ¾, 66 ¼)"

ribbing

3 ½"

2 ½"

facing, folded over and sewn to WS

25 (26 ½, 26 ½, 26 ½)"

BACK, FRONTS, AND YOKE

12 ½ (13 ½, 13 ½, 13 ½)" 7 (7 ½, 7 ½, 7 ½)"

2 ½"

6 ¾ (7 ½, 8, 9 ¼)"

FINISHING

Collar

With RS facing, pick up and knit 13 (14, 15, 17) sts along Right Front neck shaping, 12 (14, 16, 20) sts across Back neck, and 13 (14, 15, 17) sts along Left Front neck shaping–38 (42, 46, 54) sts. (WS) Begin 2×2 Rib, beginning with Row 2. Work even for 6". BO all sts loosely in pattern.

Front Bands

With RS facing, beginning at base of Collar, pick up and knit 102 (106, 106, 106) sts along Left Front edge. (WS) Begin 2×2 Rib, beginning with Row 2. Work even for 1½" or to same width as your ribbon. BO all sts loosely knitwise. Repeat for Right Front, beginning at bottom edge.

Cut 2 lengths of ribbon long enough to fit Front Bands, plus ¼" at each end for finishing. Using sewing thread, sew ribbon to RS of Left Front Band, folding ¼" of ribbon to WS at each end for a neat edge. Repeat for Right Front Band, sewing ribbon to WS of Band. Mark snap placement along Front Bands, with first snap ½" below Collar and last snap 2" above bottom of Band, and remaining snaps evenly spaced between. Sew on snaps.

Arm Slit Facings: Fold far right-hand and far left-hand arm slit facings to WS of piece and sew to WS along 3 edges of facings, being careful not to let sts show on RS. Slip center right-hand and center left-hand facings into arm slits, without folding, and sew CO and BO edges to folded facings. Cut 2 lengths of ribbon long enough to fit around inside of arm slits, plus ¼" of ribbon at each end for finishing. Beginning at top of arm slit, using sewing thread, sew ribbon to facings on inside of arm slit, folding ¼" of ribbon to WS at each end for a neat edge.

Block as desired.

MAKE IT YOUR OWN

Instead of the collar shown, you can work a Mandarin collar and give it a more elegant look. How would you do this? Well, just follow the directions for picking up the stitches around the neckline edges, but instead of working the knit 2, purl 2 rib, work a different edging, like Seed stitch or even Garter stitch, and work even for a couple of inches before binding off. You may find that you have to go down several needle sizes in order to give the collar enough body to stand up (if the yarn you are using is soft and drapey, it may not be appropriate for a Mandarin collar). To complete the Asian feel, use frog closures instead of snaps and embellish the button bands with a silk ribbon. But do plan ahead and work the bottom edges of the cape in the same edging you choose for your collar.

CHAPTER 3

Top-Down Set-In Sleeve Sweaters

Sweaters with set-in sleeves are desirable (to me, anyway) because of the way they fit in the shoulder area—the edges of the armhole and the top of the garment fall at or near the shoulder line and fit together perfectly.

The garments in this chapter are all worked in one piece from the top down and have what look to be set-in sleeves—that is, rather than sewing in the sleeves as you would with the pattern piece approach, stitches are picked up around the armhole and worked down to the cuff. These afterthought sleeves (as I like to call them) can be added once the body is complete. Because you're picking up stitches around the armhole, you won't have to sew in the sleeves later, so your sleeves will look professionally finished and totally fab. If you are new to top-down, set-in sleeve sweaters, check out Tang on page 56 to learn the basics.

SIZES

X-Small (Small, Medium, Large, 1X-Large, 2X-Large, 3X-Large)

FINISHED MEASUREMENTS

30¼ (34¾, 38¼, 42¾, 46¼, 50¾, 54¼)" chest

YARN

Malabrigo Kettle-Dyed Merino (100% merino wool; 216 yards / 100 grams): 5 (6, 6, 7, 8, 9, 9) hanks #194 cinnabar

NEEDLES

One 32" (82 cm) long or longer circular (circ) needle size US 7 (4.5 mm)

One 16" (40 cm) long circ needle size US 7 (4.5 mm)

One 16" (40 cm) long circ needle size US 8 (5 mm)

One or two 24" (60 cm) long or longer circ needles or one set of five double-pointed needles (dpn) size US 7 (4.5 mm), as preferred, for Sleeves

Change needle size if necessary to obtain correct gauge.

NOTIONS

Waste yarn; removable marker; stitch markers in 3 colors

GAUGE

18 sts and 22 rows = 4" (10 cm) in Stockinette stitch (St st)

TANG

In its most basic form, Tang is a seamless, top-down, sleeveless shell. Then add afterthought sleeves, starting at the armhole and working down to the cuff. Once you understand how this type of sweater is constructed, your mind will open up to all sorts of design opportunities that will personalize the garment even more.

BACK

Note: After the initial Provisional CO, use Backward Loop CO for any other COs in this pattern (see Special Techniques, page 162). Using 32" long circ needle, waste yarn and Provisional CO, CO 60 (64, 68, 72, 78, 82, 84) sts. (RS) Change to working yarn; begin St st. Work even until piece measures 6 (6 ½, 6 ½, 7 ¼, 7 ½, 7 ½, 8)" from the beginning, ending with a WS row.

Shape Armholes (RS): Increase 1 st each side this row, then every other row 0 (0, 1, 1, 2, 2, 2) time(s), as follows: K1, m1, work to last st, m1, k1–62 (66, 72, 76, 84, 88, 90) sts. Work even for 1 row.

Next Row (RS): CO 1 (3, 3, 5, 5, 6, 7) sts at beginning of next 2 rows, then 2 (3, 4, 5, 5, 7, 9) sts at beginning of next 2 rows–68 (78, 86, 96, 104, 114, 122) sts. Transfer sts to waste yarn for Body.

FRONT

With RS facing, carefully unravel Provisional CO and place first and last 20 (22, 22, 24, 26, 26, 28) sts on 32" long circ needle for Fronts. Transfer remaining center 20 (20, 24, 24, 26, 30, 28) sts to waste yarn for Back neck. Place removable marker for top of shoulder. (RS) Working BOTH SIDES AT SAME TIME using separate balls of yarn, begin St st. Work even for 8 rows.

> PATTERN FEATURES
> Top-down set-in sleeve construction, body and sleeves worked in the round, provisional cast-on, short-row shaping

STITCH PATTERN

3×1 Rib
(multiple of 4 sts; 1-rnd repeat)
All Rnds: *K3, p1; repeat from * around.

Shape Neck (RS): Increase 1 st each neck edge this row, then every other row 4 (4, 5, 5, 6, 7, 7) times, as follows: On right Front, work to last st, m1, k1; on left Front, k1, m1, work to end—25 (27, 28, 30, 33, 34, 36) sts each Front. Work even for 1 row.

Next Row (RS): Work across right Front, CO 10 (10, 12, 12, 12, 14, 12) sts for center neck, work across left Front to end, cutting second ball of yarn—60 (64, 68, 72, 78, 82, 84) sts for Front. Work even until piece measures same as for Back from top of shoulder to beginning of armhole shaping, ending with a WS row. Shape armholes as for Back—68 (78, 86, 96, 104, 114, 122) sts.

BODY

Join Back and Front (RS): Work across Front sts, pm, work across Back sts from waste yarn—136 (156, 172, 192, 208, 228, 244) sts. *Note: The Back sts referred to are the sts that were placed on waste yarn after working the armhole shaping, not the Back neck sts that were placed on waste yarn after unraveling the Provisional CO. Join for working in the rnd; pm for beginning of rnd. Work even until piece measures 11 (11½, 12¼, 12½, 13, 13¼, 13½)" from top of shoulder.*

Shape Waist

Decrease Rnd: Decrease 4 sts this rnd, then every 6 rnds twice, as follows: K1, k2tog, work to 3 sts before next marker, ssk, k1, slip marker (sm), k1, k2tog, work to 3 sts before next marker, ssk, k1—124 (144, 160, 180, 196, 216, 232) sts remain. Work even for 6 rnds.

Increase Rnd: Increase 4 sts this rnd, then every 6 rnds twice, as follows: K1, m1, work to 1 st before next marker,

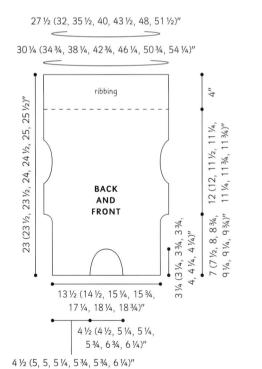

27½ (32, 35½, 40, 43½, 48, 51½)"

30¼ (34¾, 38¼, 42¾, 46¼, 50¾, 54¼)"

ribbing

BACK
AND
FRONT

23 (23½, 23½, 24, 24½, 25, 25½)"

4"

12 (12, 11½, 11¼, 11¾)" 9¼, 9¼, 9¾)"

7 (7½, 8, 8¾, 9¼, 9¼, 9¾)"

3¼ (3¼, 3¾, 3¾, 4, 4¼, 4¼)"

13½ (14½, 15¼, 15¾, 17¼, 18¼, 18¾)"

4½ (4½, 5¼, 5¼, 5¾, 6¾, 6¼)"

4½ (5, 5, 5¼, 5¾, 5¾, 6¼)"

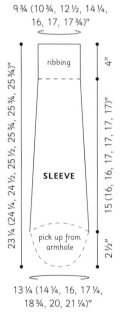

9¾ (10¾, 12½, 14¼, 16, 17, 17¾)"

ribbing

SLEEVE

pick up from armhole

23¼ (24¼, 24½, 25½, 25¾, 25¾, 25¾)"

4"

15 (16, 16, 17, 17, 17, 17)"

2½"

13¼ (14¼, 16, 17¼, 18¾, 20, 21¼)"

m1, k1, sm, k1, m1, work to 1 st before next marker, m1, k1—136 (156, 172, 192, 208, 228, 244) sts. Work even until piece measures 19 (19½, 19½, 20, 20½, 21, 21½)" from top of shoulder.

Next Rnd: Change to 3×1 Rib. Work even for 4". BO all sts loosely in pattern.

SLEEVES

Note: Use your preferred method of working in the rnd when working the Sleeves (see page 150). You will be using 3 different color markers: 1 color for beginning of rnd, 2 of color A to mark end of cap shaping, and 2 of color B to mark center of cap shaping.

With RS facing, beginning at bottom center of underarm, pick up and knit 60 (64, 72, 78, 84, 90, 96) sts as follows: 7 (8, 11, 13, 15, 17, 19) sts, pm color A, 13 sts, pm color B, 20 (22, 24, 26, 28, 30, 32) sts, pm color B, 13 sts, pm color A, 7 (8, 11, 13, 15, 17, 19) sts.
Note: Be sure to pick up the same number of sts between bottom center of armhole and top of shoulder on both sides of the armhole. Color B markers should be equidistant from top of shoulder. If you would prefer not to place markers while you pick up sts, you may first pick up the total number of sts required, join for working in the rnd, then knit 1 rnd, placing the markers according to the numbers given in the pick-up instructions.

Shape Cap

Note: Cap will be shaped using Short Rows (see Special Techniques, page 162). Hide wraps as you come to them.

Row 1: Working back and forth, begin St st. Work to second color B marker, sm, wrp-t.

Row 2: Repeat Row 1.

Row 3: Work to wrapped st of row before last row worked, work wrapped st, work 1 st, wrp-t.

Repeat Row 3 until you have reached the color A markers on each side of Sleeve.

Next Rnd (RS): Change to working in the rnd, hiding remaining wrap as you come to it, and removing all markers; pm for beginning of rnd. Work even for 6 rnds.

Shape Sleeve: Decrease 2 sts this rnd, every 6 (6, 4, 4, 4, 4, 4) rnds 7 (4, 10, 10, 11, 12, 9) times, then every 0 (4, 2, 2, 2, 2, 2) rnds 0 (5, 3, 6, 8, 10, 16) times, as follows: K1, k2tog, work to last 3 sts, ssk, k1—44 sts remain. Work even until piece measures 15 (16, 16, 17, 17, 17, 17)", measuring from bottom center of underarm, or to 4" from desired length.

Next Rnd: Change to 3×1 Rib. Work even for 4". BO all sts loosely in pattern.

FINISHING

Turtleneck: With RS facing, using smaller 16" long circ needle, work across sts on waste yarn for Back neck, pick up and knit approximately 1 st for each row or st around neck shaping, ending with a multiple of 4 sts. Join for working in the rnd; pm for beginning of rnd. Begin 3×1 Rib. Work even for 4". Change to larger 16" long circ needle; work even until Turtleneck measures 7½" from pick-up rnd. BO all sts loosely in pattern.

Block as desired.

MAKE IT YOUR OWN

Want a crewneck instead of a turtleneck? Simply pick up stitches around the neck edges, work the edging of your choice for an inch, and bind off. Sleeves can also be altered on the fly if you want a shorter or capped sleeve instead (see Adjusting Shaping, page 148).

SIZES

X-Small (Small, Medium, Large, 1X-Large, 2X-Large, 3X-Large)

FINISHED MEASUREMENTS

30 ¼ (33 ¾, 36 ½, 40, 44, 49 ¼, 52 ½)" chest

YARN

Cascade Yarns Cascade 220 The Heathers (100% Peruvian Highland wool; 220 yards / 100 grams): 4 (4, 5, 5, 6, 6, 7) hanks #2440

NEEDLES

One 32" (82 cm) long or longer circular (circ) needle size US 7 (4.5 mm)

One 16" (40 cm) long circ needle size US 7 (4.5 mm) (for sizes 2X-Large and 3X-Large)

One or two 24" (60 cm) long or longer circ needles or one set of five double-pointed needles (dpn) size US 7 (4.5 mm), as preferred, for Sleeves

Change needle size if necessary to obtain correct gauge.

NOTIONS

Waste yarn; removable markers; stitch markers in 3 colors; 1½ (1½, 2, 2, 2½, 2½, 2½) yards [or double bust measurement] ¾" wide ribbon to match

GAUGE

18 sts and 22 rows = 4" (10 cm) in Seed stitch

JANE

Jane is a cardigan that can be customized in so many simple ways. Just think, by dropping the eyelets and ribbon closure down a few inches to the natural waistline and lengthening the seed stitch section, you can change the focal point. And since the sleeves are worked from the top down, you can try on as you go and make a sleeveless, capped or cropped version of your own.

This garment is worked from the top of the shoulder, down the back, to the bottom of the armhole. After placing the back stitches on hold, you start at the top of the shoulders and work each front side individually until you reach the bottom of the armholes. After that, the whole piece is joined together at the sides, and you work back and forth without a care in the world (unless a 24-row stitch pattern knocks the wind out of you). My version of this cardigan has a few inches of negative ease, so when it is worn, the fronts don't quite meet in the center. Yeah, I know, it's a little edgy. But I like it this way.

PATTERN FEATURES
Top-down set-in sleeve construction, provisional cast-on, sleeves worked in the round, long-repeat stitch pattern, short-row shaping

ABBREVIATIONS

RT (Right Twist): Skip first st and knit into second st, then knit into first stitch, slipping both sts from needle together.

LT (Left Twist): Skip first st and knit into back of second st, then knit into front of first st, slipping both sts from needle together.

STITCH PATTERNS

Seed Stitch
(multiple of 2 sts; 1-row/rnd repeat)
Row/Rnd 1 (RS): *K1, p1; repeat from * to end.
Row/Rnd 2: Purl the knit sts and knit the purl sts.
Repeat Row/Rnd 2 for Seed stitch.

Brocade Chevron
(multiple of 10 sts + 4; 24-row repeat)
Note: Slip all sts purlwise with yarn in front.
Row 1 (WS): Purl.
Row 2: K1, *RT, k8; repeat from * to last 3 sts, RT, k1.
Row 3: P1, *slip 2, p8; repeat from * to last 3 sts, slip 2, p1.
Row 4: K2, *LT, k6, RT; repeat from * to last 2 sts, k2.
Row 5: K1, p1, *k1, slip 1, p6, slip 1, p1; repeat from * to last 2 sts, k1, p1.
Row 6: P1, k1, *p1, LT, k4, RT, k1; repeat from * to last 2 sts, p1, k1.
Row 7: [K1, p1] twice, *slip 1, p4, slip 1, [k1, p1] twice; repeat from * to end.
Row 8: [P1, k1] twice, *LT, k2, RT, [p1, k1] twice; repeat from * to end.

Row 9: K1, *[p1, k1] twice, slip 1, p2, slip 1, p1, k1; repeat from * to last 3 sts, p1, k1, p1.
Row 10: P1, *[k1, p1] twice, LT, RT, k1, p1; repeat from * to last 3 sts, k1, p1, k1.
Row 11: *[K1, p1] 3 times, slip 2, k1, p1; repeat from * to last 4 sts, [k1, p1] twice.
Row 12: *[P1, k1] 3 times, RT, p1, k1; repeat from * to last 4 sts, [p1, k1] twice.
Row 13: *K1, p1; repeat from * to end.
Row 14: P1, *RT, [k1, p1] 4 times; repeat from * to last 3 sts, RT, k1.
Row 15: K1, *slip 2, [p1, k1] 4 times; repeat from * to last 3 sts, slip 2, p1.
Row 16: K2, *LT, [p1, k1] 3 times, RT; repeat from * to last 2 sts, k2.
Row 17: P3, *slip 1, [k1, p1] 3 times, slip 1, p2; repeat from * to last st, p1.
Row 18: K3, *LT, [k1, p1] twice, RT, k2; repeat from * to last st, k1.
Row 19: P4, *slip 1, [p1, k1] twice, slip 1, p4; repeat from * to end.
Row 20: K4, *LT, p1, k1, RT, k4; repeat from * to end.
Row 21: P5, *slip 1, k1, p1, slip 1, p6; repeat from * to last 9 sts, slip 1, k1, p1, slip 1, p5.
Row 22: K5, *LT, RT, k6; repeat from * to last 9 sts, LT, RT, k5.
Row 23: P6, *slip 2, p8; repeat from * to last 8 sts, slip 2, p6.
Row 24: K6, *RT, k8; repeat from * to last 8 sts, RT, k6.
Repeat Rows 1-24 for Brocade Chevron.

BACK

Note: After the initial Provisional CO, use Backward Loop CO for any other CO's in this pattern (see Special Techniques, page 162). When increasing or casting on sts, work increased sts in st pattern.

Using 32″ long circ needle, waste yarn and Provisional CO, CO 60 (64, 66, 70, 72, 78, 82) sts. (RS) Change to working yarn; begin Seed st. Place removable marker at beginning of first row to mark RS. Work even until piece measures 6 (6 ½, 6 ½, 7, 7 ½, 7 ¾, 8)″ from the beginning, ending with a WS row.

Shape Armholes (RS): Increase 1 st each side this row, then every other row 0 (0, 1, 1, 2, 2, 2) time(s), as follows: K1-f/b [or p1-f/b if next st to be worked is a knit st], work to last st, p1-f/b [or k1-f/b if next st to be worked is a purl st]–62 (66, 70, 74, 78, 84, 88) sts.

Next Row (RS): CO 1 (2, 3, 4, 5, 6, 7) sts at beginning of next 2 rows, then 2 (3, 3, 4, 6, 7, 8) sts at beginning of next 2 rows–68 (76, 82, 90, 100, 110, 118) sts. Work even for 1 row. Transfer sts to waste yarn for Body. Break yarn.

FRONTS

With RS facing, carefully unravel Provisional CO and place first and last 21 (21, 23, 23, 23, 25, 25) sts on 32″ long circ needle for Fronts. Transfer remaining center 18 (22, 20, 24, 26, 28, 32) sts to waste yarn for Back neck. Place removable marker for top of shoulder. (RS) Working BOTH SIDES AT SAME TIME using separate balls of yarn, begin Seed st. Work even for 6 (6, 6, 6, 8, 8, 8) rows.

Shape Neck (RS): Increase 1 st each neck edge this row, then every other row 8 (10, 9, 11, 11, 14, 15) times, as follows: On Right Front, work to last st, p1-f/b [or k1-f/b if previous st is a purl st]; on Left Front, K1-f/b [or p1-f/b if next st to be worked is a knit st] work to end–30 (32, 33, 35, 35, 40, 41) sts each Front. Work even until piece measures same as for Back from top of shoulder to beginning of armhole shaping. Shape armholes as for Back, ending with a WS row–34 (38, 41, 45, 49, 56, 59) sts each Front. Break yarn for Right Front.

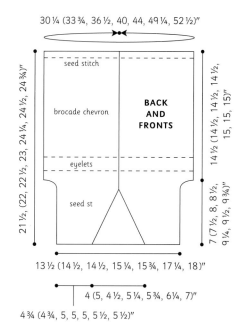

30 ¼ (33 ¾, 36 ½, 40, 44, 49 ¼, 52 ½)″

seed stitch

brocade chevron

BACK AND FRONTS

eyelets

seed st

14 ½ (14 ½, 14 ½, 14 ½, 15, 15, 15)″

7 (7 ½, 8, 8 ½, 9 ¼, 9 ½, 9 ¾)″

21 ½ (22, 22 ½, 23, 24 ¼, 24 ½, 24 ¾)″

13 ½ (14 ½, 14 ½, 15 ¼, 15 ¾, 17 ¼, 18)″

4 (5, 4 ½, 5 ¼, 5 ¾, 6 ¼, 7)″

4 ¾ (4 ¾, 5, 5, 5, 5 ½, 5 ½)″

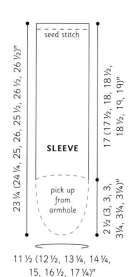

seed stitch

SLEEVE

pick up from armhole

23 ¼ (24 ¼, 25, 26, 25 ½, 26 ½, 26 ½)″

17 (17 ½, 18, 18 ½, 18 ½, 19, 19)″

2 ½ (3, 3, 3, 3 ¼, 3 ¼, 3 ¼)″

11 ½ (12 ½, 13 ¼, 14 ¼, 15, 16 ½, 17 ¼)″

BODY

Join Back to Fronts (RS): With RS facing, transfer Back sts, then Right Front sts to left-hand end of circ needle. *Note: The Back sts referred to are the sts that were placed on waste yarn after working the armhole shaping, not the Back neck sts that were placed on waste yarn after unraveling the Provisional CO.* Your sts should now be in the following order, from right to left, with RS facing: Left Front, Back, Right Front. Using yarn attached to Left Front, work across Left Front, pm for side, work across Back, pm for side, work across Right Front—136 (152, 164, 180, 198, 222, 236) sts. Do NOT join. Working back and forth, work even for 5 (5, 5, 5, 7, 7, 7) rows.

Note: The following eyelet pattern is meant to fall in the center of the bust. If you wish the pattern to fall below the bust or at the waist, continue working in Seed st to desired length before beginning the eyelet pattern.

Establish Eyelet Pattern

Row 1 (RS): Work 5 sts in Seed st, place marker (pm), knit to last 5 sts, pm, work in Seed st to end.

Row 2: Work in Seed st to first marker, purl to next marker, work in Seed st to end.

Rows 3 and 4: Repeat Row 2.

Row 5 (Eyelet Row): K2 (4, 1, 3, 3, 3, 4), *yo, k2tog, k4; repeat from * to last 2 (4, 1, 3, 3, 3, 4) sts, knit to end.

Row 6: Repeat Row 2.

Row 7: Work in Seed st to first marker, knit to next marker, work in Seed st to end.

Row 8: Repeat Row 7.

Size X-Small Only:

Next Row (RS): Work in Seed st to first marker, work in St st to next marker, decrease 2 sts evenly spaced between markers, work in Seed st to end—134 sts remain.

Sizes Small (Medium, Large, 1X-Large, 2X-Large, 3X-Large) Only:

Next Row (RS): Work in Seed st to first marker, work in St st to next marker, increase 2 (0, 4, 6, 2, 8) sts evenly spaced between markers, work in Seed st to end—154 (164, 184, 204, 224, 244) sts.

All Sizes:

Begin Brocade Chevron (WS): Work in Seed st to first marker, work in Brocade Chevron to next marker, work in Seed st to end. Work even until 3 full repeats of Brocade Chevron are complete. Piece should measure approximately 20 ½ (21, 21 ½, 22, 22 ¾, 23, 23 ¼)" from top of shoulder. *Note: For a longer cardigan, you may work additional pattern repeats, ending with Row 13 if you prefer to work a half repeat.*

(RS) Change to Seed st across all sts. Work even for 1". BO all sts loosely in pattern.

SLEEVES

Note: Use your preferred method of working in the rnd when working the Sleeves (see page 150). You will be using 3 different color markers; one color for beginning of rnd, 2 of color A to mark end of cap shaping, and 2 of color B to mark center of cap shaping.

With RS facing, beginning at bottom center of underarm, pick up and knit 52 (56, 60, 64, 68, 74, 78) sts as follows: 4 (4, 5, 6, 6, 8, 9) sts, pm color A, 13 (15, 15, 15, 17, 17, 17) sts, pm color B, 18 (18, 20, 22, 22, 24, 26) sts, pm color B, 13 (15, 15, 15, 17, 17, 17) sts, pm color A, 4 (4, 5, 6, 6, 8, 9) sts. Do NOT join. *Note: Be sure to pick up the same number of sts between bottom center of armhole and top of shoulder on both sides of the armhole. Color B markers should be equidistant from top of shoulder. If you would prefer not to place markers while you pick up sts, you may first pick up the total number of sts required, join for working in the rnd, then knit 1 rnd, placing the markers according to the numbers given in the pick-up instructions.*

Shape Cap

Note: Cap will be shaped using Short Rows (see Special Techniques, page 162). Hide wraps as you come to them.

Row 1 (RS): Working back and forth, begin St st, work to second color B marker, slip marker (sm), wrp-t.

Row 2: Repeat Row 1.

Row 3: Work to wrapped st of row below last row worked, work wrapped st, work 1 st, wrp-t.

Repeat Row 3 until you have reached the color A markers on each side of the Sleeve.

(RS) Change to working in the rnd, hiding remaining wrap as you come to it, and removing all markers; pm for beginning of rnd. Work even until piece measures 16 (16 ½, 17, 17 ½, 17 ½, 18, 18)", measuring from bottom center of underarm, or to 1" from desired length. Change to Seed st; work even for 1". BO all sts loosely in pattern.

FINISHING

Thread ribbon through eyelets. Block as desired.

MAKE IT YOUR OWN

Both versions of this pattern have an eyelet panel that is meant to fall in the center of the bust. If you want to change your design, you can continue working Seed stitch, and try on the garment periodically to move the eyelet panel down for an empire waist. You could even move the eyelet down to the waist area and work only one repeat of the Brocade Chevron for a completely different look. For the variation, I worked 3 ½ repeats of the Brocade Chevron Pattern, and threaded a leather strap through the eyelets. Seed stitch is self-finishing and won't roll, so subtract the sleeves and now you have a vest.

The sleeveless variation was worked in a size Small with 4 hanks of the same yarn used in the main version, but in color #2430. Read about estimating yarn requirements on page 160.

SADDLE A-LINE

There aren't a lot of saddle shoulder sweater patterns out and about these days, so I figure it's about time to add one to the mix—but this time, top down and in the round. The "saddle" part of this sweater is a strip of knitting that runs from the neck edge at the top of the shoulder, all the way down the sleeve. Some people work the sleeves the usual way—as separate pieces, starting at the cuff and working up toward the shoulder and neck—but picture the sleeve with that saddle portion at the top and consider how you'd ever manage to sew it into the armhole without clearing out the liquor cabinet or calling up a seamstress.

Instead, what you will do in this pattern is start by casting on approximately 2 or 3 inches worth of stitches at the top of each shoulder and knitting a strip ("saddle") long enough to reach from the neck to the shoulder edge. Don't bind off on either side—just leave the live stitches on waste yarn or a stitch holder so they'll be available when you pick them up later for the sleeves, thus allowing your saddle to smoothly transition from shoulder to sleeve.

PATTERN FEATURES
Top-down set-in sleeve construction, body and sleeves worked in the round, provisional cast-on, cables, short-row shaping

SIZES
X-Small (Small, Medium, Large, 1X-Large, 2X-Large, 3X-Large)

FINISHED MEASUREMENTS
30¾ (34, 37¼, 42, 46, 50, 54)" chest

YARN
Blue Sky Alpacas Alpaca Silk (50% alpaca / 50% silk; 146 yards / 50 grams): 6 (6, 7, 7, 8, 9, 10) hanks #123 ruby

NEEDLES
One set of five double-pointed needles (dpn) size US 5 (3.75 mm)

Two 29" (74 cm) long or longer circular (circ) needles size US 5 (3.75 mm)

One 16" (40 cm) long circ needle size US 3 (3.25 mm)

One 16" (40 cm) long circ needle size US 5 (3.75 mm)

One or two 24" (60 cm) long or longer circ needles or one set of five dpn size US 5 (3.75 mm), as preferred, for Sleeves

Change needle size if necessary to obtain correct gauge.

NOTIONS
Stitch markers in 3 colors; waste yarn; removable marker

GAUGE
24 sts and 28 rows = 4" (10 cm) in Stockinette stitch (St st) using larger needles

STITCH PATTERNS

Slipped Chain Cable A
(panel of 10 sts; 8-row repeat)
Rows 1 and 5 (WS): K2, p6, k2.
Row 2: P2, slip 1 wyib, k4, slip 1 wyib, p2.
Row 3: K2, slip 1 wyif, p4, slip 1 wyif, k2.
Row 4: P2, drop slipped st of previous row to front of work, k2, pick up dropped st and knit it, slip 2 wyib, drop slipped st of previous row to front of work, slip the 2 slipped sts from right-hand needle back to left-hand needle, pick up dropped st and knit it, k2, p2.
Row 6: P2, k2, slip 2 wyib, k2, p2.
Row 7: K2, p2, slip 2 wyif, p2, k2.
Row 8: P2, slip 2 wyib, drop slipped st of previous row to front of work, slip the 2 slipped sts from right-hand needle back to left-hand needle, pick up dropped st and knit it, k2, drop slipped st of previous row to front of work, k2, pick up dropped st and knit it, p2.
Repeat Rows 1–8 for Slipped Chain Cable A.

Slipped Chain Cable B
(panel of 10 sts; 8-rnd repeat)
Rnds 1 and 5: P2, k6, p2.
Rnds 2 and 3: P2, slip 1 wyib, k4, slip 1 wyib, p2.
Rnd 4: P2, drop slipped st from previous rnd to front of work, k2, pick up dropped st and knit it, slip 2 wyib, drop slipped st from previous rnd to front of work, slip the 2 slipped sts from right-hand needle back to left-hand needle, pick up dropped st and knit it, k2, p2.
Rnds 6 and 7: P2, k2, slip 2 wyib, k2, p2.
Rnd 8: P2, slip 2 wyib, drop slipped st from previous rnd to front of work, slip the 2 slipped sts from right-hand needle back to left-hand needle, pick up dropped st and knit it, k2, drop slipped st from previous rnd to front of work, k2, pick up dropped st and knit it, p2.
Repeat Rnds 1–8 for Slipped Chain Cable B.

1×1 Rib
(multiple of 2 sts; 1-rnd repeat)
All Rnds: *K1, p1; repeat from * around.

SADDLES (make 2)

With larger dpn, CO 14 (14, 14, 14, 16, 16, 16) sts.

Begin Pattern

Set-Up Row (RS): K2 (2, 2, 2, 3, 3, 3), place marker (pm), k10, pm, knit to end.

Row 1: Purl to marker, slip marker (sm), work in Slipped Chain Cable A across center 10 sts, purl to end.

Row 2: Knit to marker, sm, work in Slipped Chain Cable A to next marker, knit to end.

Work even until piece measures 4 ½ (4 ¾, 4 ¾, 5 ¼, 5 ¾, 5 ¾, 6)″ from the beginning, ending with a WS row. Break yarn; transfer sts and markers to waste yarn, making note of final row number so you can resume stitch pattern when you pick up sts for Sleeve at a later time.

BACK

With RS of one Saddle facing, using 29″ long circ needle, pick up and knit 27 (29, 29, 32, 35, 35, 36) sts along long side of Saddle, beginning at live st edge, and ending at CO edge; using Backward Loop CO (see Special Techniques, page 162), CO 26 (26, 28, 32, 32, 34, 36) sts for center Back neck; with RS of second Saddle facing, pick up and knit 27 (29, 29, 32, 35, 35, 36) sts along long side of Saddle, beginning at CO edge and ending at live st edge—80 (84, 86, 96, 102, 104, 108) sts. Begin St st; work even until armhole measures 5 (5, 5, 5 ½, 5 ½, 5 ¾, 6)″ from pick-up row, ending with a WS row.

Shape Armhole (RS): Increase 1 st each side this row, then every other row 1 (1, 3, 3, 3, 3, 4) time(s), as follows: K1, m1, work to last stitch, m1, k1—84 (88, 94, 104, 110, 112, 118) sts. Work even for 1 row.

Next Row (RS): CO 2 (3, 4, 5, 6, 5, 6) sts at beginning of next 2 rows, 2 (4, 5, 6, 8, 6, 7) sts at beginning of next 2 rows, then 0 (0, 0, 0, 0, 8, 9) sts at beginning of next 2 rows—92 (102, 112, 126, 138, 150, 162) sts. Transfer sts to waste yarn.

FRONT

Work as for Back to end of armhole shaping—92 (102, 112, 126, 138, 150, 162) sts. Place removable marker on Front to differentiate it from Back.

BODY

Join Back and Front

Transfer Back sts to second 29" long circ needle. With RS of Front facing, k5, pm color A for beginning of rnd, work to last 5 sts of Front, pm color B, work to end of Front, work 5 sts of Back, pm color B for beginning of Cable, work to last 5 sts of Back, pm color B, work to end of Back, join for working in the rnd, work 5 sts of Front to end of rnd—184 (204, 224, 252, 276, 300, 324) sts.

Establish Pattern: [Work to color B marker, sm, work Slipped Chain Cable B across next 10 sts, sm] twice. Work even until piece measures 2 ¼ (2 ¾, 2 ¾, 3 ¼, 4 ¼, 4, 3 ¾)" from armhole.

Shape Waist

Set-Up Rnd: Continuing as established, work 18 (20, 24, 26, 30, 32, 36) sts, pm color C, work 46 (52, 54, 64, 68, 76, 80) sts, pm color C, work 46 (50, 58, 62, 70, 74, 82) sts, pm color C, work 46 (52, 54, 64, 68, 76, 80) sts, pm color C, work to end.

Decrease Rnd: Decrease 4 sts this rnd, then every 3 rnds 3 times, as follows: [Work to 2 sts before next color C marker, ssk, sm, work to next color C marker, sm, k2tog] twice, work to end—168 (188, 208, 236, 260, 284, 308) sts remain. Work even for 8 rnds.

Increase Rnd: Increase 8 sts this rnd, then every 7 (7, 8, 9, 9, 9, 9) rnds 8 (8, 7, 6, 5, 5, 5) times, as follows: [Work to next marker, m1, sm, work to next marker, sm, m1, work to next marker, sm, m1-p, work to next marker, m1-p, sm] twice—240 (260, 272, 292, 308, 332, 356) sts. *Note: Purl increased sts between color B markers at left side and color B and A markers at right and knit increased sts on either side of color C markers.* Work even until piece measures 14 ½ (15, 15, 15, 15, 15 ¼, 15 ¼)" from armhole.

Next Rnd: Change to 1×1 Rib; work even for 1". BO all sts loosely in pattern.

SLEEVES

Note: Use your preferred method of working in the rnd when working the Sleeves (see page 150). You will be using 3 different color markers: 1 of color C for beginning of rnd, 2 of color A to mark end of cap shaping, and 2 of color B to mark center of cap shaping.

Transfer 1 set of Saddle sts to larger needle(s). With RS facing, beginning at bottom center of underarm and ending right before Saddle, pick up and knit 32 (35, 41, 46, 48, 52, 57) sts as follows: 11 (13, 19, 22, 24, 27, 32) sts, pm color A, 15 (15, 13, 13, 13, 13, 11) sts, pm color B, 6 (7, 9, 11, 11, 12, 14) sts; work across 14 (14, 14, 14, 16, 16, 16) Saddle sts, continuing in Slipped Chain

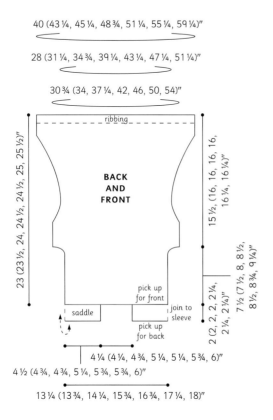

40 (43 ¼, 45 ¼, 48 ¾, 51 ¼, 55 ¼, 59 ¼)″

28 (31 ¼, 34 ¾, 39 ¼, 43 ¼, 47 ¼, 51 ¼)″

30 ¾ (34, 37 ¼, 42, 46, 50, 54)″

ribbing

BACK AND FRONT

23 (23 ½, 24, 24 ½, 24 ½, 25, 25 ½)″

15 ½, (16, 16, 16, 16, 16, 16 ¼)″

pick up for front

join to sleeve

saddle

pick up for back

7 ½ (7 ½, 8, 8 ½, 8 ½, 8 ¾, 9 ¼)″

2 (2, 2, 2 ¼, 2 ¼, 2 ½)″

4 ¼ (4 ¼, 4 ¾, 5 ¼, 5 ¼, 5 ¾, 6)″

4 ½ (4 ¾, 4 ¾, 5 ¼, 5 ¾, 5 ¾, 6)″

13 ¼ (13 ¾, 14 ¼, 15 ¾, 16 ¾, 17 ¼, 18)″

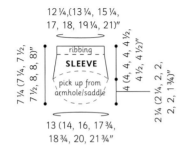

12 ¼,(13 ¼, 15 ¼, 17, 18, 19 ¼, 21)″

ribbing
SLEEVE
pick up from armhole/saddle

7 ¼ (7 ¼, 7 ½, 7 ½, 8, 8, 8)″

4 (4, 4, 4, 4 ½, 4 ½)″

2 ¼ (2 ¼, 2, 2, 2, 1 ¾)″

13 (14, 16, 17 ¾, 18 ¾, 20, 21 ¾)″

Cable as established; beginning at end of Saddle and ending at bottom center of underarm, pick up and knit 32 (35, 41, 46, 48, 52, 57 sts as follows: 6 (7, 9, 11, 11, 12, 14) sts, pm color B, 15 (15, 13, 13, 13, 13, 11) sts, pm color A, 11 (13, 19, 22, 24, 27, 32) sts, pm color C for beginning of rnd—78 (84, 96, 106, 112, 120, 130) sts total. *Note: If you would prefer not to place markers while you pick up sts, you may first pick up the total number of sts required, working across the Saddle as indicated. Be sure to pick up the same number of sts between bottom center of armhole and the Saddle on both sides of the armhole. Color B markers should be equidistant from top of shoulder. Join for working in the rnd, then knit 1 rnd, working Saddle sts in Slipped Chain Cable as established, placing the markers according to the numbers given in the pick-up instructions.*

Shape Cap

Note: Cap will be shaped using Short Rows (see Special Techniques, page 162). Hide wraps as you come to them.

Row 1: Working back and forth in St st on either side of Saddle sts, and in Slipped Chain Cable as established over Saddle sts, work to second color B marker, sm, wrp-t.

Row 2: Repeat Row 1.

Row 3: Work to wrapped st of row before last row worked, work wrapped st, work 1 st, wrp-t.

Repeat Row 3 until you have reached color A markers on each side of Sleeve.

Next Rnd (RS): Change to working in the rnd, hiding remaining wrap as you come to it, and removing all markers; pm for beginning of rnd. Work even for 6 rnds.

Shape Sleeve: Decrease 2 sts this rnd, then every 7 rnds once, as follows: K1, k2tog, work to last 3 sts, ssk, k1—74 (80, 92, 102, 108, 116, 126) sts remain. Work even until piece measures 3 (3, 3, 3, 3 ½, 3 ½, 3 ½)″ from pick-up rnd, measuring from bottom center of underarm.

Change to smaller needle(s) and 1×1 Rib; work even for 1″. BO all sts loosely.

FINISHING

Turtleneck

With RS facing, using smaller 16″ long circ needle, beginning at Back neck, pick up and knit an even number of sts around neck edge, keeping in mind that Turtleneck will have to fit over your head. Join for working in the rnd; pm for beginning of rnd. Begin 1×1 Rib; work even for 4″. Change to larger 16″ long circ needle; work even for 1″. BO all sts loosely in pattern.

Block as desired, making sure Cable panels lay flat.

MAKE IT YOUR OWN

Want a crewneck saddle sweater without the A-line shaping like the one shown here? Work the waist shaping as you normally would, increasing for the hips at color C markers until it just fits. A good rule of thumb is to work the same number of increase rounds for the hips as you did decrease rounds for the waist, omitting the additional hip increases on either side of the cables that give the main pattern its A-line shape. The crewneck collar shown here is worked just like the one in the main pattern, but for only 2″ before binding off. Fold the neckline edging to the inside, and sew it down along the inside neck edge. Work the Sleeves for 2″ before changing to ribbing.

This variation was worked in a size Small with 7 hanks of Blue Sky Alpacas Mélange (100% baby alpaca; 110 yards / 50 grams) color #5471. See page 160 for information on estimating yarn requirements.

X-Small (Small, Medium, Large,
1X-Large, 2X-Large, 3X-Large)

FINISHED MEASUREMENTS

29¾ (31¼, 35¾, 38½, 43, 47¼,
53)" chest

*Note: This is a stretchy sweater;
allow for at least 2" or more of
negative ease for a fit like the
one shown here.*

YARN

RYC Cashsoft Baby DK (57%
extrafine merino / 33% microfiber /
10% cashmere; 142 yards / 50
grams): 4 (4, 5, 5, 6, 6, 7) balls
#807 pixie

NEEDLES

One 32" (82 cm) long or longer
circ needle size US 6 (4 mm)

One 32" (82 cm) long or longer
circular (circ) needle size US 4
(3.5 mm)

One or two 24" (60 cm) long or
longer circ needles or one set of
five dpn size US 6 (4 mm), as
preferred, for Sleeves

One or two 24" (60 cm) long or
longer circ needles or one set of
five double-pointed needles (dpn)
size US 4 (3.5 mm), as preferred,
for Sleeves

Change needle size if necessary
to obtain correct gauge.

NOTIONS

Waste yarn; removable marker;
stitch markers in 3 colors; eight
to ten clear snaps; eight to ten
½" buttons (optional); 2 yards
⅞"-wide grosgrain ribbon;
matching sewing thread; sewing
needle

GAUGE

22 sts and 28 rows = 4" (10 cm)
in Broken Rib Stitch using larger
needles

CAMEO

Sometimes there's nothing better than a little cardigan you can throw on in a pinch, something that serves you for more than one season and looks smart and finished, even though it's handmade. The ribbon along the button band is a sweet surprise, while the simple stitch pattern adds a bit of fun. This cardigan is intentionally close-fitting and cropped.

BACK

Note: Keep first and last st of every row in St st. After the initial Provisional CO, use Backward Loop CO for any other COs in this pattern (see Special Techniques, page 162). When increasing or casting on sts, work increased sts in st pattern.

Using larger 32" long circ needle, waste yarn and Provisional CO, CO 72 (76, 80, 88, 92, 96, 104) sts. (RS) Change to working yarn; k1 (edge st, keep in St st), work Broken Rib Stitch to last st, k1 (edge st, keep in St st). Work even until piece measures 5 ½ (5 ¾, 6 ¼, 6 ½, 7, 7 ½, 8 ½)" from the beginning, ending with a WS row.

Shape Armholes (RS): Increase 1 st each side this row, then every other row once, as follows: K1-f/b, work to last st, k1-f/b—76 (80, 84, 92, 96, 100, 108) sts. Work even for 1 row. *Note: Keep track of what row number of the*

Broken Rib Stitch you ended on before beginning armhole shaping; you will need it when you work the armhole shaping for the Front.

Next Row (RS): CO 1 (1, 2, 2, 5, 6, 9) sts, work to end, CO 1 (1, 2, 2, 5, 6, 9) sts—78 (82, 88, 96, 106, 112, 126) sts. Work even for 1 row.

Next Row (RS): CO 1 (1, 4, 4, 5, 8, 9) sts, work to end, CO 1 (1, 4, 4, 5, 8, 9) sts—80 (84, 96, 104, 116, 128, 144) sts. Work even for 1 row, working first and last sts in St st. Transfer sts to waste yarn for Body. Break yarn.

FRONTS

With RS facing, carefully unravel Provisional CO and place first and last 16 (16, 20, 24, 24, 28, 32) sts on circ needle for Fronts. Transfer remaining center 40 (44, 40, 40, 44, 40, 40) sts to waste yarn for Back neck. Place removable marker for top of shoulder.

PATTERN FEATURES
Top-down set-in sleeve construction, sleeves worked in the round, provisional cast-on, short-repeat stitch pattern, short-row shaping, ribbon and snaps sewn on using a needle and thread

STITCH PATTERNS

Broken Rib Stitch

(multiple of 4 sts + 2; 12-row repeat)

Row 1 (RS): K2, *p2, k2; repeat from * to end.

Rows 2, 4, 6, 7, 9, and 11: P2, *k2, p2; repeat from * to end.

Rows 3, 5, 8, 10, and 12: Repeat Row 1.

Repeat Rows 1-12 for Broken Rib Stitch.

2×2 Rib

(multiple of 4 sts + 2; 2-row repeat)

Row 1 (RS): K2, *p2, k2; repeat from * to end.

Row 2: P2, *k2, p2; repeat from * to end.

Repeat Rows 1 and 2 for 2×2 Rib.

(RS) Working BOTH SIDES AT SAME TIME using separate balls of yarn, k1 (edge st, keep in St st), beginning with Row 7 of pattern, work in Broken Rib Stitch to last st, k1 (edge st, keep in St st). Work even for 5 rows.

Next Row (RS): On Right Front, work to end, CO 22 (24, 22, 22, 24, 22, 22) sts; on Left Front, CO 22 (24, 22, 22, 24, 22, 22) sts, work to end—38 (40, 42, 46, 48, 50, 54) sts each Front. Working edge sts in St st, work even in pattern until piece measures same as for Back from top of shoulder to beginning of armhole shaping, ending with a WS row. *Note: To ensure that the pattern flows correctly when Back and Fronts are joined, if you ended the Back on Row 2, 4, 6, 8, 10, or 12 before working the armhole shaping, you should end here with Row 8, 10, 12, 2, 4, or 6 respectively.* Shape armholes as for Back, ending with a WS row—42 (44, 50, 54, 60, 66, 74) sts each Front. Break yarn for Right Front.

BODY

Join Back to Fronts (RS): With RS facing, transfer Back sts, then Right Front sts to left-hand end of circ needle. *Note: The Back sts referred to are the sts that were placed on waste yarn after working the armhole shaping, not the Back neck sts that were placed on waste yarn after unraveling the Provisional CO.* Your sts should now be in the following order, from right to left, with RS facing: Left Front, Back, Right Front. Using yarn attached to Left Front, work across Left Front, work across Back, work across Right Front—164 (172, 196, 212, 236, 260,

292) sts. Do NOT join. Working back and forth, keeping first and last st of every row in St st, work even until piece measures 16 ½ (16 ½, 17, 18, 19, 19, 19 ½)" from top of shoulder, ending with Row 12 or 6 of pattern.

Next Row (RS): Change to smaller circ needle, k1 (edge st, keep in St st), purl the knit sts and knit the purl sts as they face you to last st, k1 (edge st, keep in St st).

Next Row (WS): Working first and last sts in St st, knit the knit sts and purl the purl sts as they face you. Repeat last row 12 times. BO all sts loosely in pattern.

SLEEVES

Note: Use your preferred method of working in the rnd when working the Sleeves (see page 150). You will be using 3 different color markers; one color for beginning of rnd, 2 of color A to mark end of cap shaping, and 2 of color B to mark center of cap shaping.

With RS facing, using larger needle(s), beginning at bottom center of underarm, pick up and knit 56 (60, 68, 72, 80, 88, 92) sts as follows: 2 (3, 4, 5, 6, 8, 6), pm color A, 17 (17, 19, 19, 21, 21, 25) sts, pm color B, 18 (20, 22, 24, 26, 30, 30) sts, pm color B, 17 (17, 19, 19, 21, 21, 25) sts, pm color A, 2 (3, 4, 5, 6, 8, 6) sts. *Note: Be sure to pick up the same number of sts between bottom center of armhole and top of shoulder on both sides of the armhole. Color B markers should be equidistant from top of shoulder. If you would prefer not to place markers while you pick up sts, you may first pick up the total number of sts required, join for working in the rnd, then knit 1 rnd, placing the markers according to the numbers given in the pick-up instructions.*

Shape Cap

Note: Cap will be shaped using Short Rows (see page 162).

Rows 1 (RS) and 2: Working back and forth, begin St st. Work to second color B marker, slip marker (sm), wrp-t.

Row 3: Work to wrapped st of row before last row worked, work wrapped st, work 1 st, wrp-t.

Repeat Row 3 until you have reached color A markers on each side of Sleeve, ending with a WS row.

Next Rnd (RS): Change to working in the rnd, hiding remaining wrap as you come to it, and removing all markers; pm for beginning of rnd. Work even for 4 rnds.

Shape Sleeve: Decrease 2 sts this rnd, then every 3 rnds once, as follows: K1, k2tog, work to last 3 sts, ssk, k1—52 (56, 64, 68, 76, 84, 88) sts remain. Change to smaller needle(s) and 2×2 Rib; work even for 7 rnds. BO all sts loosely knitwise.

FINISHING

Front Bands: With RS facing, using smaller needle, pick up and knit approximately 3 sts for every 4 rows along Right Front edge, ending with a multiple of 4 sts + 2. (WS) Begin 2×2 Rib, beginning with Row 2. Work even for 7 rows. BO all sts knitwise. Repeat for Left Front edge.

Collar (*Note: Collar is worked in 3 separate pieces.*)

Front Collar: With RS facing, using smaller needles, beginning at top of Right Front Band, and ending before the 6 rows worked at top of shoulder, pick up and knit sts across Band and sts CO at top of Front, ending with a multiple of 4 sts + 2. (WS) Begin 2×2 Rib, beginning with Row 2. Work even for 7 rows. BO all sts loosely in pattern. Repeat for Left Front.

Back Collar: Transfer sts from waste yarn to smaller needle. With WS facing, join yarn. Begin 2×2 Rib. Work even for 7 rows. BO all sts loosely in pattern.

Sew side edges of Front Collars to edges of first 6 rows at top of shoulder. Sew side edges of Back Collar to edges of Front Collars on WS.

Cut 2 lengths of ribbon long enough to fit Front Bands, plus ¼" at each end for finishing. Using thread, sew ribbon to RS of Left Front Band, ending below neck edging, folding ¼" of ribbon to WS at each end for a neat edge. Repeat for Right Front Band, sewing ribbon to WS of Band. Mark snap placement along Front Bands, with first snap ½" below Collar and last snap ½" above bottom of Band, and remaining snaps evenly spaced between. Sew on snaps. Sew 8 to 10 buttons along RS of Right Front Band (optional) in same positions as snaps. Block as desired.

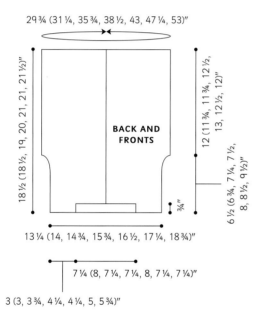

29¾ (31¼, 35¾, 38½, 43, 47¼, 53)"

BACK AND FRONTS

18½ (18½, 19, 20, 21, 21, 21½)"

12 (11¾, 11¾, 12½, 13, 12½, 12)"

6½ (6¾, 7¼, 7½, 8, 8½, 9½)"

¾"

13¼ (14, 14¾, 15¾, 16½, 17¼, 18¾)"

7¼ (8, 7¼, 7¼, 8, 7¼, 7¼)"

3 (3, 3¾, 4¼, 4¼, 5, 5¾)"

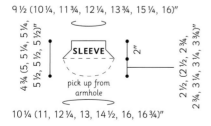

9½ (10¼, 11¾, 12¼, 13¾, 15¼, 16)"

4¾ (5, 5¼, 5¼, 5½, 5½, 5½)"

SLEEVE

2"

pick up from armhole

2½ (2½, 2¾, 2¾, 3¼, 3½, 3¾)"

10¼ (11, 12¼, 13, 14½, 16, 16¾)"

MAKE IT YOUR OWN

If you want to simplify matters, work your sweater in allover Stockinette stitch instead of Broken Rib Stitch (but make sure that you match the gauge given for the Broken Rib Stitch). Sleeves can be easily changed, so work them to whatever length you like, adding sleeve shaping as necessary (see Adjusting Shaping, page 148). And if a cropped sweater isn't for you, make sure you have enough yarn (see page 160), and keep knitting until it's your perfect length.

SIZES

X-Small (Small, Medium, Large, 1X-Large, 2X-Large, 3X-Large)

FINISHED MEASURMENTS

29 (33½, 36¼, 42¼, 46½, 49½, 53¾)" chest

YARN

Elsebeth Lavold Silky Wool (65% wool / 35% silk; 192 yards / 50 grams): 4 (4, 5, 6, 7, 7, 8) hanks #17 sandstone

NEEDLES

One 29" (74 cm) long or longer circular (circ) needle size US 6 (4 mm)

One 29" (74 cm) long circ needle size US 4 (3.5 mm)

One or two 24" (60 cm) long or longer circ needles or one set of five double-pointed needles (dpn) size US 6 (4 mm), as preferred, for Sleeves

One or two 24" (60 cm) long or longer circ needles or one set of five dpn size US 4 (3.5 mm), as preferred, for Sleeves

Change needle size if necessary to obtain correct gauge.

NOTIONS

Waste yarn; stitch markers in 3 colors; removable stitch marker; five ¼" buttons

GAUGE

22 sts and 28 rows = 4" (10 cm) in 2×2 Rib, slightly stretched, using larger needles

SLINKY RIBS

One of the things that has always bothered me about hand-knit ribbed sweaters—particularly ones that are knit in pieces—is that it's just about impossible for me to make the ribs fit into the armhole correctly. Honestly, I think you have to be an expert knitter and seamstress, and maybe even some kind of a magician, if you want to end up with a sweater that can be worn out of doors without drawing a few curious stares. But I tell you, the clouds parted and the angels sang for me when I learned how to work a top-down seamless sleeve. When worked this way, the lines of a ribbed sleeve flow effortlessly off of the shoulder and out of the armhole, yielding very professional-looking results.

> PATTERN FEATURES
> Top-down set-in sleeve construction, body and sleeves worked in the round, provisional cast-on, short-row shaping

STITCH PATTERN

2×2 Rib

(multiple of 4 sts; 1-row repeat)

Row 1 (RS): *K2, p2; repeat from * to end, end k2 if necessary.

Row 2: Knit the knit sts and purl the purl sts as they face you.

Repeat Row 2 for 2×2 Rib.

BACK

Note: After the initial Provisional CO, use Backward Loop CO for any other COs in this pattern (see Special Techniques, page 162). When increasing or casting on sts, work increased sts in st pattern. Using larger 29" long circ needle, waste yarn and Provisional CO, CO 70 (78, 86, 86, 94, 94, 94) sts. (RS) Change to working yarn, begin 2×2 Rib. Work even until piece measures 6 (6, 6¼, 6¾, 6¾, 7, 7½)" from the beginning, ending with a WS row. Place removable marker on first row to indicate RS.

Shape Armholes (RS): Increase 1 st each side this row, then every other row 1 (1, 2, 2, 2, 2, 2) time(s), as follows: K1-f/b, work to last st, k1-f/b–74 (82, 92, 92, 100, 100, 100) sts. Work even for 1 row.

Next Row (RS): CO 1 (2, 2, 4, 4, 6, 8) sts, work to end, CO 1 (2, 2, 4, 4, 6, 8) sts–76 (86, 96, 100, 108, 112, 116) sts. Work even for 1 row.

Next Row (RS): CO 2 (3, 2, 4, 5, 6, 8) sts, work to end, CO 2 (3, 2, 4, 5, 6, 8) sts–80 (92, 100, 108, 118, 124, 132) sts. Work even for 1 row.

Sizes Large, 1X-Large, 2X-Large, and 3X-Large Only:

Next Row (RS): CO 4 (5, 6, 8) sts, work to end, CO 4 (5, 6, 8) sts–116 (128, 136, 148) sts. Work even for 1 row.

All Sizes:

Transfer sts to waste yarn for Body. Break yarn.

FRONT

With RS facing, carefully unravel Provisional CO and place first and last 20 (24, 24, 24, 28, 28, 28) sts on larger 29" long circ needle for Front. Transfer remaining center 30 (30, 38, 38, 38, 38, 38) sts to waste yarn for Back neck. Place removable marker for top of shoulder. (RS) Working BOTH SIDES AT SAME TIME using separate balls of yarn, begin 2×2 Rib as follows: On Right Front, *k2, p2; repeat from * to end; on Left Front, *p2, k2; repeat from * to end. When piece measures 6 (6, 6¼, 6¾, 6¾, 7, 7½)" from top of shoulder, ending with a WS row, shape armholes as for Back, ending with a WS row–25 (31, 31, 39, 45, 49, 55) sts each side. Break yarn for Right Front.

BODY

Join Back to Fronts

With RS facing, transfer Back sts, then Right Front sts to left-hand end of circ needle. *Note: The Back sts referred to are the sts that were placed on waste yarn after working the armhole shaping, not the Back neck sts that were placed on waste yarn after unraveling the Provisional CO.* Your sts should now be in the following order, from right to left, with RS facing: Left Front, Back, Right Front. Using yarn attached to Left Front, work across Left Front, pm for left side, work across Back, pm for right side, work across Right Front–130 (154, 162, 194, 218, 234, 258) sts. Do NOT join. Working back and forth, work even for 1 row.

Shape Neck (RS): Increase 1 st each side this row, then every other row once, as follows: K1-f/b [or p1-f/b if first st to be worked is a purl st], work to last st, k1-f/b [or p1-f/b]–134 (158, 166, 198, 222, 238, 262) sts. Work even for 1 row.

Next Row (RS): CO 6 (6, 8, 8, 8, 8, 8) sts, work to end, CO 6 (6, 8, 8, 8, 8, 8) sts–146 (170, 182, 214, 238, 254, 278) sts. Work even for 1 row.

Next Row (RS): CO 6 (6, 8, 8, 8, 8, 8) sts, work to end, CO 6 (6, 8, 8, 8, 8, 8) sts–158 (182, 198, 230, 254, 270, 294) sts. Work even until piece measures 10¾ (10¾, 11, 11¾, 11¾, 12, 12½)" from top of shoulder, ending with a WS row.

Join Fronts

Next Row (RS): Work to end, CO 2 sts–160 (184, 200, 232, 256, 272, 296) sts. Join for working in the rnd; work to second marker [this will now be beginning of rnd marker]. Work even for 4 rnds.

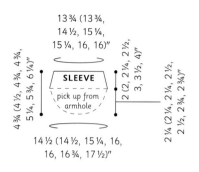

13 ¾ (13 ¾, 14 ½, 15 ¼, 15 ¼, 16, 16)"

SLEEVE
pick up from armhole

4 ¾ (4 ½, 4 ¾, 4 ¾, 5 ¼, 5 ¾, 6 ¼)"

2 (2, 2 ¼, 2 ½, 3, 3 ½, 4)"

2 ¼ (2 ¼, 2 ¼, 2 ½, 2 ½, 2 ¾, 2 ¾)"

14 ½ (14 ½, 15 ¼, 16, 16, 16 ¾, 17 ½)"

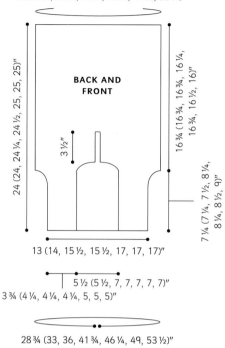

29 (33 ½, 36 ¼, 42 ¼, 46 ½, 49 ½, 53 ¾)"

BACK AND FRONT

16 ¾ (16 ¾, 16 ¾, 16 ¼, 16 ¾, 16 ½, 16)"

24 (24, 24 ¼, 24 ½, 25, 25, 25)"

3 ½"

7 ¼ (7 ¼, 7 ½, 8 ¼, 8 ¼, 8 ½, 9)"

13 (14, 15 ½, 15 ½, 17, 17, 17)"

5 ½ (5 ½, 7, 7, 7, 7, 7)"

3 ¾ (4 ¼, 4 ¼, 4 ¼, 5, 5, 5)"

28 ¾ (33, 36, 41 ¾, 46 ¼, 49, 53 ½)"

Work Rib Detail 1: Work 3 (5, 1, 5, 3, 7, 1) sts, k4, *p2, k6; repeat from * to last 1 (7, 3, 7, 1, 5, 3) sts, p1 (2, 2, 2, 1, 2, 2), k0 (5, 1, 5, 0, 4, 1). *Note: Size 2X-Large will overlap next rnd by 1 st. Do not reposition beginning of rnd marker.* Work even for 7 rnds.

Sizes Small (Medium, Large, 3X-Large):

Work Rib Detail 2: Work 9 (13, 5, 5) sts, k8, [p2, k14] 1 (1, 2, 3) times, p2, k22, *p2, k14; repeat from * to last 15 (11, 3, 3) sts, p2, k13 (9, 1, 1).

Sizes X-Small (1X-Large, 2X-Large):

Work Rib Detail 2: Work 7 (15, 2) sts, k8, *p2, k14; repeat from * to last 1 (9, 5) sts, p1 (2, 2), k0 (8, 3). *Note: Size 1X-Large will overlap next rnd by 1 st. Do not reposition beginning of rnd marker.*

All Sizes:

Work even for 7 rnds.

Next Rnd: Change to St st. Work even until piece measures 23 ½ (23 ½, 23 ¾, 24, 24 ½, 24 ½, 24 ½)"

from top of shoulder, or to desired length minus ½". Purl 1 rnd.

Next Rnd: Change to smaller 29" long needle. Work even for 6 rnds. BO all sts loosely. *Note: BO edge will roll slightly. If you would prefer that the edge not roll, you may fold it to WS at purl rnd and sew to WS, being careful not to let sts show on RS.*

SLEEVES

Note: Use your preferred method of working in the rnd when working the Sleeves (see page 150). You will be using 3 different color markers: 1 color for beginning of rnd, 2 of color A to mark end of cap shaping, and 2 of color B to mark center of cap shaping.

With RS facing, using larger needle(s) beginning and ending at center underarm, pick up and knit 80 (80, 84, 88, 88, 92, 96) sts as follows: 12 (12, 13, 12, 12, 12, 13) sts, pm color A, 15 (15, 15, 17, 17, 19, 19) sts, pm color B, 26 (26, 28, 30, 30, 30, 32) sts, pm color B, 15 (15, 15, 17, 17, 19, 19) sts, pm color A, 12 (12, 13, 12,

12, 12, 13) sts. Do NOT join. *Note: Be sure to pick up the same number of sts between bottom center of armhole and top of shoulder on both sides of the armhole. Color B markers should be equidistant from top of shoulder. If you would prefer not to place markers while you pick up sts, you may first pick up the total number of sts required, join for working in the rnd, then knit 1 rnd, placing the markers according to the numbers given in the pick-up instructions.*

Shape Cap

Note: Cap will be shaped using Short Rows (see Special Techniques, page 162). Hide wraps as you come to them.

Row 1: Begin 2×2 Rib as follows: K1, p2, *k2, p2; repeat from * to last st, k1.

Rows 2 and 3: Continuing in pattern, work to second color B marker, sm, wrp-t.

Row 4: Work to wrapped st of row before last row worked, work wrapped st, work 1 st, wrp-t.

Repeat Row 4 until you have reached the color A markers on each side of Sleeve.

Next Rnd (RS): Change to working in the rnd, hiding remaining wrap as you come to it, and removing all markers; pm for beginning of rnd.

Shape Sleeve: Decrease 2 sts this rnd, then every 7 rnds 1 (1, 1, 1, 1, 3) time(s), as follows: Ssk, work to last 2 sts, k2tog—76 (76, 80, 84, 84, 86, 88) sts remain. Work even until Sleeve measures 1 (1, 1¼, 1½, 2, 2½, 3)" from underarm, or to 1" less than desired length, measuring from bottom center of underarm. Change to smaller needle(s). Work even for 1". BO all sts loosely in pattern.

FINISHING

Button Bands: With RS facing, using smaller needle, beginning at center of left Front, where Fronts are joined, pick up and knit approximately 2 sts for every 3 rows along Left Front edge. Begin St st. Work even for 3 rows. BO all sts loosely. Repeat for opposite side. Sew lower right-hand edge of right Button Band to WS of 2 CO sts at center Front; sew lower left-hand edge of left Button Band to WS of right Button Band.

MAKE IT YOUR OWN

The best thing about working sleeves top-down is that once you finish the shaping at the top, you can keep working, round and round, until the length is just right for you. For a shallower neckline, (shown unbuttoned on the variation here), work to 1" before where you want the bottom of your neck shaping to be. Work the neck shaping on the Fronts as given in the pattern (under Body), then work to the required length to begin the armhole shaping. Complete the pattern as written, omitting the neck shaping. Work the Sleeves until they reach your wrist, adding shaping as necessary (see page 148). Rib the entire length of the Sleeve, if you want, or, like the one here, work the body rib pattern to the middle of the Sleeve, change to Stockinette stitch (knit all rounds), and then about ½" before you're done, work a purl round, knit a few rounds, then bind off so the Sleeve edge looks the same as the body.

This variation was worked in a size X-Small with 6 hanks of the same yarn used for the main version, but in color #16. Read about estimating yarn requirements on page 160.

Neckband: Transfer Back neck sts from waste yarn to spare needle. With RS facing, using smaller circ needle, beginning at top edge of right Button Band, pick up and knit approximately 2 sts for every 3 rows to Back, knit across Back neck sts, pick up and knit approximately 2 sts for every 3 rows to top edge of left Button Band. Begin St st. Work even for 3 rows. BO all sts loosely. Sew buttons, evenly spaced, to left Button Band and Neckband; push buttons through right Button Band and Neckband.

Block as desired.

LETTUCE COAT

Deceptively quick to knit in a lofty yarn, this funky coat is a perfect project for someone who is looking for warmth, without the weight of a typical knitted coat. If you're concerned about knitting such a large object in one piece, have no worries. Just find a drawstring plastic bag or a large laundry bag, and when the body is finished and you're working the sleeves, carefully place the finished part of the coat in the bag, cinch it slightly, and complete your sleeve outside the bag. This will both protect the coat and keep it from getting unwieldy while you're working.

The width across the Back is a little narrower than your average sweater, and the bottom of the sweater and the sleeves are worked in brioche rib stitch, the thicker fabric adding some interest and warmth. Applied I-cords serve as button loops at the sleeve cuffs and as closures on the bodice.

PATTERN FEATURES
Top-down set-in sleeve construction, sleeves worked in the round, provisional cast-on, brioche stitch pattern, applied I-Cord edging

SIZES
X-Small (Small, Medium, Large, 1X-Large, 2X-Large, 3X-Large)

FINISHED MEASUREMENTS
32 (35½, 40, 43½, 48, 51½, 56)" chest

YARN
Malabrigo Kettle-Dyed Merino (100% merino wool; 216 yards / 100 grams): 6 (6, 7, 7, 8, 9, 10) hanks #37 lettuce

NEEDLES
One 32" (82 cm) long or longer circular (circ) needle size US 9 (5.5 mm)

One 16" (40 cm) long circ needle size US 9 (5.5 mm)

One 16" (40 cm) long circ needle size US 8 (5 mm)

One or two 24" (60 cm) long or longer circ needles or one set of five double-pointed needles (dpn) size US 8 (5 mm), as preferred, for Sleeves

One or two 24" (60 cm) long or longer circ needles or one set of five dpn size US 9 (5.5 mm), as preferred, for Sleeves

Change needle size if necessary to obtain correct gauge.

NOTIONS
Waste yarn; removable marker; stitch markers in 3 colors; six ⅞" buttons; four 1⅛" buttons

GAUGE
14 sts and 20 rows = 4" (10 cm) in Stockinette stitch (St st) using larger needle

18 sts and 23 rows = 4" (10 cm) in St st using smaller needle

STITCH PATTERN

Brioche Rib

(multiple of 2 sts; 1-row repeat)

Note: This pattern may begin on a RS or WS row.

Row 1 (Set-Up Row): *Yo, slip 1, k1; repeat from * to end.

Row 2: *Yo, slip 1, k2tog (slipped st and yo); repeat from * to end.

Repeat Row 2 for Brioche Rib.

BACK

Note: After the initial Provisional CO, use Backward Loop CO for any other COs in this pattern (see Special Techniques, page 162). Using 32" long circ needle, waste yarn and Provisional CO, CO 44 (46, 50, 52, 56, 58, 60) sts. Change to working yarn, begin St st. Work even until piece measures 5¾ (5¾, 6¼, 6¾, 7, 7¾, 8¾)" from the beginning, ending with a WS row.

Shape Armholes (RS): Increase 1 st each side this row, then every other row once—48 (50, 54, 56, 60, 62, 64) sts. Work even for 1 row.

Next Row (RS): CO 2 (3, 4, 4, 6, 6, 8) sts, work to end, CO 2 (3, 4, 4, 6, 6, 8) sts—52 (56, 62, 64, 72, 74, 80) sts. Work even for 1 row.

Next Row (RS): CO 2 (3, 4, 6, 6, 8, 9) sts, work to end, CO 2 (3, 4, 6, 6, 8, 9) sts—56 (62, 70, 76, 84, 90, 98) sts. Work even for 1 row. Transfer sts to waste yarn for Body.

FRONT

With RS facing, carefully unravel Provisional CO and place first and last 14 (14, 16, 16, 16, 18, 20) sts on 32" long circ needle for Fronts. Transfer remaining center 16 (18, 18, 20, 24, 22, 20) sts to waste yarn for Back neck. Place removable marker for top of shoulder. (RS) Working BOTH SIDES AT SAME TIME, work even until piece measures 1½ (1½, 2, 2, 2, 2, 2)" from top of shoulder, ending with a WS row.

Shape Neck (RS): Increase 1 st each neck edge this row, then every other row 2 (3, 3, 4, 4, 4, 4) times, as follows: On Right Front, work to last st, m1, k1; on Left Front, k1, m1, work to end—17 (18, 20, 21, 21, 23, 25) sts. Work even for 1 row.

Next Row (RS): On Right Front, work to end, CO 5 (5, 5, 5, 7, 6, 5) sts; on Left Front, CO 5 (5, 5, 5, 7, 6, 5) sts, work to end—22 (23, 25, 26, 28, 29, 30) sts each Front. Work even until piece measures same as for Back to beginning of armhole shaping, ending with a WS row. Shape armholes as for Back, ending with a WS row—28 (31, 35, 38, 42, 45, 49) sts each Front. Break yarn for Right Front.

BODY

Join Back to Fronts (RS): With RS facing, transfer Back sts, then Right Front sts to left-hand end of circ needle. *Note: The Back sts referred to are the sts that were placed on waste yarn after working the armhole shaping, not the Back neck sts that were placed on waste yarn after unraveling the Provisional CO.* Your sts should now be in the following order, from right to left, with RS facing: Left Front, Back, Right Front. Using yarn attached to Left Front, work across Left Front, pm for left side, work across Back, pm for right side, work across Right Front—112 (124, 140, 152, 168, 180, 196) sts. Do NOT join. Working back and forth, work even for 11 rows.

Shape Waist (RS): Decrease 4 sts this row, then every 4 rows twice, as follows: [Work to 3 sts before next marker, ssk, k1, sm, k1, k2tog] twice, work to end—100 (112, 128, 140, 156, 168, 184) sts remain. Work even until piece measures 12½ (12½, 13, 13½, 14, 14¼, 14½)" from top of shoulder, ending with a WS row.

Next Row (RS): Change to Brioche Rib. Work even until piece measures 30 (30, 30½, 31, 31½, 31¾, 32)" from top of shoulder, ending with a RS row.

Next Row (WS): *P1, k2tog (slipped st and yo); repeat from * to end. BO all sts loosely in 1×1 Rib as follows: P1, k1, BO 1 st, *p1, BO 1 st, k1, BO 1 st; repeat from * to end.

SLEEVES

Note: Use your preferred method of working in the rnd when working the Sleeves (see page 150). You will be using 3 different color markers; one color for beginning of rnd, 2 of color A to mark end of cap shaping, and 2 of color B to mark center of cap shaping.

With RS facing, using smaller needle(s), beginning at bottom center of underarm, pick up and knit 52 (56, 62, 68, 74, 82, 92) sts as follows: 6 (8, 10, 10, 12, 14, 16) sts, pm color A, 11 (11, 11, 13, 13, 13, 15) sts, pm color B, 18 (18, 20, 22, 24, 28, 30) sts, pm color B, 11 (11, 11, 13, 13, 13, 15) sts, pm color A, 6 (8, 10, 10, 12, 14, 16) sts. *Note: Be sure to pick up the same number of sts*

between bottom center of armhole and top of shoulder on both sides of the armhole. Color B markers should be equidistant from top of shoulder. If you would prefer not to place markers while you pick up sts, you may first pick up the total number of sts required, join for working in the rnd, then knit 1 rnd, placing the markers according to the numbers given in the pick-up instructions.

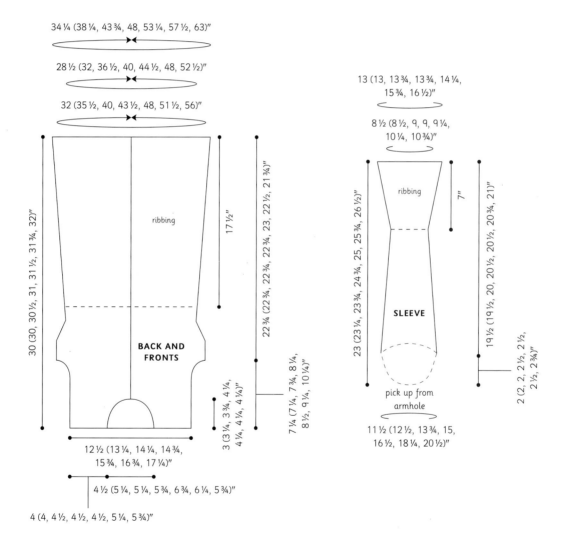

34 ¼ (38 ¼, 43 ¾, 48, 53 ¼, 57 ½, 63)″

28 ½ (32, 36 ½, 40, 44 ½, 48, 52 ½)″

32 (35 ½, 40, 43 ½, 48, 51 ½, 56)″

ribbing

BACK AND FRONTS

30 (30, 30 ½, 31, 31 ½, 31 ¾, 32)″

17 ½″

22 ¾ (22 ¾, 22 ¾, 22 ¾, 23, 22 ½, 21 ¾)″

3 (3 ¼, 3 ¾, 4 ¼, 4 ¼, 4 ¼, 4 ¼)″

7 ¼ (7 ¼, 7 ¾, 8 ¼, 8 ½, 9 ¼, 10 ¼)″

12 ½ (13 ¼, 14 ¼, 14 ¾, 15 ¾, 16 ¾, 17 ¼)″

4 ½ (5 ¼, 5 ¼, 5 ¾, 6 ¾, 6 ¼, 5 ¾)″

4 (4, 4 ½, 4 ½, 4 ½, 5 ¼, 5 ¾)″

13 (13, 13 ¾, 13 ¾, 14 ¼, 15 ¾, 16 ½)″

8 ½ (8 ½, 9, 9, 9 ¼, 10 ¼, 10 ¾)″

ribbing

SLEEVE

pick up from armhole

23 (23 ¼, 23 ¾, 24 ¾, 25, 25 ¾, 26 ½)″

7″

19 ½ (19 ½, 20, 20 ½, 20 ½, 20 ¾, 21)″

2 (2, 2, 2 ½, 2 ½, 2 ½, 2 ¾)″

11 ½ (12 ½, 13 ¾, 15, 16 ½, 18 ¼, 20 ½)″

Shape Cap

Note: Cap will be shaped using Short Rows (see Special Techniques, page 162). Hide wraps as you come to them.

Row 1 (RS): Working back and forth, begin St st. Work to second color B marker, slip marker (sm), wrp-t.

Row 2: Repeat Row 1.

Row 3: Work to wrapped st of row before last row worked, work wrapped st, work 1 st, wrp-t.

Repeat Row 3 until you have reached the color A markers on each side of Sleeve, ending with a WS row.

Next Rnd (RS): Change to working in the rnd, hiding remaining wrap as you come to it, and removing all markers; pm for beginning of rnd. Work even for 5 rnds.

Shape Sleeve: Decrease 2 sts this rnd, every 6 rnds 6 (3, 1, 0, 0, 0, 0) time(s), every 4 rnds 0 (5, 9, 8, 6, 4, 2) times, then every other rnd 0 (0, 0, 5, 9, 13, 19) times, as follows: K1, k2tog, work to last 3 sts, ssk, k1—38 (38, 40, 40, 42, 46, 48) sts remain. Work even until piece measures 12½ (12½, 13, 13½, 13½, 13¾, 14)″ from pick-up rnd, measuring from bottom center of armhole.

Next Rnd: Change to larger needle(s), work 19 (19, 20, 20, 21, 23, 24) sts, turn work.

Begin Cuff (WS): Change to Brioche Rib. Work even until piece measures 19½ (19½, 20, 20½, 20½, 20¾, 21)″ from pick-up row, measuring from bottom center of armhole, ending with a RS row.

Next Row (WS): *P1, k2tog (slipped st and yo); repeat from * to end. BO all sts loosely as for Body.

FINISHING

Front I-Cord Edging: Place markers for 4 larger buttons along Left Front, the first 1″ below neck shaping, the last 1″ above ribbing, and the remaining 2 evenly spaced between. Place markers for button loops along Right Front, opposite button markers on Left Front. Using smaller dpn, CO 2 sts. With RS facing, beginning at end of neck shaping, work Attached I-Cord (see Special Techniques, page 162) along Left Front. Work Attached I-Cord along Right Front as for Left Front, beginning at bottom edge, and working button loops at each marker as follows: Work to marker, work 4 rows of straight (unattached) I-Cord without picking up any sts, work next row of Attached I-Cord, picking up new st 1 row above last picked-up st. *Note: If you are using a button that is extra large, consider working your next pick-up 2 rows above the last picked-up st, so that the button will fit through the loop.*

Sleeve I-Cord Edging: Place markers for 3 smaller buttons along left edge of Right Sleeve Cuff slit, the first 1″ below beginning of slit, the last 1″ above BO edge, and the remaining 1 evenly spaced between. Place markers for button loops along right edge, opposite button markers on left edge. Using smaller dpn, CO 2 sts. With RS facing, beginning at left edge of Sleeve Cuff, work Attached I-Cord along both sides of slit, working button loops at each loop marker as for Front Edging. Work Edging on Left Sleeve Cuff as for Right Sleeve Cuff, placing button markers along right edge of Sleeve Cuff slit and button loop markers along left edge.

COLLAR

Transfer Back neck sts from waste yarn to spare needle. With RS facing, using smaller circ needle, pick up an even number of sts along Right Front neck shaping, including I-Cord Edging, knit across Back neck sts, pick up and knit an even number of sts along Left Front neck shaping, including I-Cord Edging. (WS) Begin Brioche Rib. Work even for 1½″, ending with a RS row.

Next Row (WS): *P1, k2tog (slipped st and yo); repeat from * to end. BO all sts loosely as for Body.

Sew larger buttons on Left Front at button markers. Sew smaller buttons on Sleeves at button markers.

Block as desired.

MAKE IT YOUR OWN

If you're hankering for a wider collar—one that folds over and lays flat over the shoulders—simply work the collar as directed, but keep going until it just reaches the shoulder seam when folded over. To make the collar lie down nicely, change to larger needles and work a few extra rows. Bind off very loosely. Length can also be a variable here, and you could easily make a cardigan rather than a coat by knitting it to a shorter length.

JEWEL

If you're looking for a straightforward shell pattern with just a few bells and whistles, yet with enough pizzazz to keep your knitting interesting, this is the shell for you. Featuring a fun jewel-like ribbing along the boat neck and hem, this little number also has some nifty dartlike shaping instead of the usual side shaping that many knitting patterns seem to have.

And if you want to add even more challenge and shape to your own version of Jewel, check out the variation to this pattern on page 91, which features short rows that subtly sculpt the neckline a little differently than the main version.

SIZES
X-Small (Small, Medium, Large, 1X-Large, 2X-Large, 3X-Large)

FINISHED MEASUREMENTS
30½ (34½, 38½, 42½, 46½, 50½, 54½)" chest

YARN
Artyarns Regal Silk (100% silk; 163 yards / 50 grams): 4 (4, 5, 5, 6, 7, 7) hanks #119

NEEDLES
One 24" (60 cm) long or longer circular (circ) needle size US 7 (4.5 mm)

Change needle size if necessary to obtain correct gauge.

NOTIONS
Crochet hook size US F/5 (3.75 mm); stitch markers in 2 colors; waste yarn

GAUGE
20 sts and 26 rows = 4" (10 cm) in Stockinette stitch (St st)

BACK

CO 70 (74, 82, 86, 90, 94, 98) sts. Begin Hourglass Rib. Work even for 28 rows [you should have completed 7 vertical repeats of Hourglass Rib].

Next Row (WS): Change to St st, slipping first st of every row purlwise. Work even until piece measures 6 (6 ½, 6 ½, 7 ¼, 7 ½, 7 ½, 8)" from the beginning, ending with a WS row.

Shape Armholes (RS): K1, m1, work to last st, m1, k1–72 (76, 84, 88, 92, 96, 100) sts. Work even for 1 row.

Next Row (RS): CO 1 (2, 3, 4, 5, 7, 9) sts at beginning of next 2 rows, then 1 (3, 3, 5, 7, 8, 9) sts at beginning of next 2 rows–76 (86, 96, 106, 116, 126, 136) sts. Transfer sts to waste yarn for Body.

> **PATTERN FEATURES**
> Top-down construction, body worked in the round, short-repeat stitch pattern, short-row shaping (variation), crab stitch edging with crochet hook

STITCH PATTERNS

Hourglass Rib

(multiple of 4 sts + 2; 4-row repeat)

Note: One st is increased per repeat on Row 3.
The original number of sts is restored on Row 4.

Row 1 (WS): K2 *p2, k2; repeat from * to end.
Row 2: P2, *k2tog-tbl but do not drop sts from left-hand needle, k2tog same 2 sts, slip both sts from left-hand needle together, p2; repeat from * to end.
Row 3: K2 *p1, yo, p1, k2; repeat from * to end.
Row 4: P2, *skp, k1, p2; repeat from * to end.
Repeat Rows 1-4 for Hourglass Rib.

Crab Stitch Edging

Row 1 (Single Crochet): Work from right to left for right-handers, or from left to right for left-handers. Make a slipknot and place on hook. *Insert hook into next st (along lower or upper edge) or between two rows (side edges). Yo hook, pull through to RS—2 loops on hook. Yo hook, draw through both loops—1 loop on hook. Repeat from * to end. Do NOT turn work. *Note: It may be necessary to skip a row every so often when working along a side edge, in order to prevent puckering.*
Row 2 (Reverse Single Crochet): Work from left to right for right-handers, or from right to left for left-handers. *Ch 1, insert hook into previous single crochet, yo hook, pull through to RS—2 loops on hook. Yo hook, draw through both loops—1 loop on hook. Repeat from * to end. Fasten off.

FRONT

Work as for Back; do NOT transfer sts to waste yarn.

BODY

Join Back and Front: With RS of Back and Front facing, transfer sts for Back to left-hand end of needle. Work across Front sts, place marker (pm) color A for side, work across Back sts—152 (172, 192, 212, 232, 252, 272) sts. Join for working in the rnd; pm color A for beginning of rnd. Work even until piece measures 10½ (11, 11½, 12½, 13½, 13½, 14)" from the beginning.

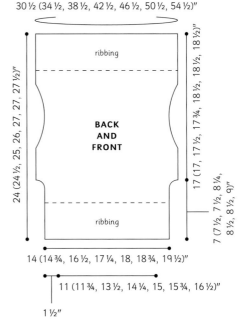

15 ½ (17 ¼, 19 ½, 21 ¼, 23 ½, 25 ¼, 27 ½)"

27 ¼ (31 ¼, 35 ¼, 39 ¼, 43 ¼, 47 ¼, 51 ¼)"

30 ½ (34 ½, 38 ½, 42 ½, 46 ½, 50 ½, 54 ½)"

ribbing

BACK AND FRONT

ribbing

24 (24 ½, 25, 26, 27, 27, 27 ½)"

17 (17, 17 ½, 17 ¾, 18 ½, 18 ½, 18 ½)"

7 (7 ½, 7 ½, 8 ¼, 8 ½, 8 ½, 9)"

14 (14 ¾, 16 ½, 17 ¼, 18, 18 ¾, 19 ½)"

11 (11 ¾, 13 ½, 14 ¼, 15, 15 ¾, 16 ½)"

1 ½"

Shape Waist

Set-Up Rnd: *Work 19 (22, 24, 27, 29, 32, 34) sts, pm color B for waist, work 38 (42, 48, 52, 58, 62, 68) sts, pm color B*, work to color A marker, slip marker (sm), repeat from * to *, work to end.

Decrease Rnd: Decrease 4 sts this rnd, then every 6 rnds 3 times, as follows: [Work to 2 sts before next color B marker, ssk, sm, work to next color B marker, sm, k2tog] twice, work to end—136 (156, 176, 196, 216, 236, 256) sts remain. Work even for 5 rnds.

Increase Rnd: Increase 4 sts this rnd, then every 6 rnds 3 times, as follows: [Work to next color B marker, m1, sm, work to next color B marker, sm, m1] twice, work to end—152 (172, 192, 212, 232, 252, 272) sts. Work even until piece measures 20 (20½, 21, 22, 23, 23, 23½)", removing color B markers on first rnd, and increasing 4 (0, 4, 0, 4, 0, 4) sts evenly spaced on last rnd—156 (172, 196, 212, 236, 252, 276) sts.

Next Rnd: Work to first marker, transfer next 78 (86, 106, 118, 126, 138) sts to waste yarn for Back—78 (86, 98, 106, 118, 126, 138) sts remain.

Next Row (WS): Working back and forth and slipping first stitch of every row purlwise, begin Hourglass Rib. *Note: The slipped st is the first st of the pattern, so on WS rows, you will work slip 1, k1, at the beginning of the row, instead of k2, and on RS rows, you will work slip 1, p1 at the beginning of the row, instead of p2.* Work even for 28 rows. BO all sts loosely in pattern.

Transfer sts for Back to needle and complete as for Front.

FINISHING

Sew shoulder seam for approximately 1½″ in from each armhole edge, or to desired shoulder width.

Armhole Edging: Using crochet hook, beginning at bottom center of underarm, work Crab Stitch Edging around armhole.

Block as desired.

MAKE IT YOUR OWN

I added short rows (see Special Techniques, page 162) at the top of the front section of this variation to create a sexy neckline that drapes forward a bit. To do this, work 5 repeats of the Hourglass Rib at the top of the Front and Back of the shell, then work short rows on the Front section only, as follows: On the first right-side row of Stockinette stitch following the Hourglass Rib, work 10 stitches, place marker, work to 10 stitches before the end, place marker and work to the end. Work 1 wrong-side row. *Note: Hide wraps as you come to them.*

Row 1 (RS): Work to furthest marker, slip marker (sm), wrp-t.
Row 2: Work to next marker, sm, wrp-t.
Rows 3 and 4: Work to 3 sts before wrapped st of row before last row worked, wrp-t.
Repeat Rows 3 and 4 four times.
Work to end, and continue working the Front, hiding the remaining wrap as you come to it. When you're ready to work the bottom edge, work only 5 repeats of the Hourglass Rib just as you did with the top.

This variation was worked in size X-Small with 3 skeins of Tilli Tomas Pure & Simple (100% spun silk; 260 yards / 100 grams) in color #394-D jade. Read about estimating yarn requirements on page 160.

SIZES

X-Small (Small, Medium, Large,
1X-Large, 2X-Large, 3X-Large)

FINISHED MEASUREMENTS

30¼ (32¼, 36¼, 38¼, 42¼,
46¼, 50¼)" chest

YARN

Dale of Norway Svale (50%
cotton / 40% viscose / 10% silk;
114 yards / 50 grams); 5 (5, 6, 6,
7, 8, 8) balls #9451 sagebrush

NEEDLES

One 32" (82 cm) long or longer
circular (circ) needle size US 5
(3.75 mm)

One 32" (82 cm) long or longer
circ needle size US 4 (3.5 mm)

One 16" (40 cm) long circ needle
size US 4 (3.5 mm)

Change needle size if necessary
to obtain correct gauge.

NOTIONS

Crochet hook size US G/6 (4
mm); waste yarn; removable
marker; stitch markers; three
⁷⁄₁₆" buttons; tapestry needle
(optional)

GAUGE

22 sts and 28 rows = 4" (10cm)
in Twisted Stockinette stitch
(Twisted St st) using larger
needles

MINA'S TUXEDO VEST

I have a dear friend, Mina, who voraciously clips inspirational photos from magazines—pictures of garments, funky jewelry, and color combinations that capture her imagination. So when I told her about this book, it's no wonder she had tons of clippings to share with me. One evening she showed me a picture of a vest that she liked, and said, "Don't you think it would be more fun with a tuxedo collar? And instead of those chunky armhole edgings, maybe something really simple?"

I agreed, and here it is.

PATTERN FEATURES
Top-down construction, provisional cast-on, short-row shaping, crab stitch edging with crochet hook

---

STITCH PATTERNS

Twisted Stockinette Stitch
(any number of sts; 2-row repeat)
Row 1 (RS): *K1-tbl; repeat from * to end.
Row 2: Purl.
Repeat Rows 1 and 2 for Twisted St st.

2×2 Rib
(multiple of 4 sts + 2; 2-row repeat)
Row 1 (RS): K2, *p2, k2; repeat from * to end.
Row 2: P2, *k2, p2; repeat from * to end.
Repeat Rows 1 and 2 for 2×2 Rib.

Crab Stitch Edging
Row 1 (Single Crochet): Make a slipknot and place on hook. *Insert hook into next st. Yo hook, pull through to RS—2 loops on hook. Yo hook, draw through both loops—1 loop on hook. Repeat from * to end. *Note: It may be necessary to skip a row every so often, in order to prevent puckering.* Do NOT turn work.
Row 2 (Reverse Single Crochet): *Ch1, insert hook into next single crochet to the right, yo hook, pull through to RS—2 loops on hook. Yo hook, draw through both loops—1 loop on hook. Repeat from * to opposite first buttonhole marker. Chain 2 (chain 3 for larger buttons), skip next 2 single crochets to the right, repeat from *, working 2 more button loops opposite buttonhole markers. Fasten off.

BACK

Note: After the initial Provisional CO, use Backward Loop CO for any other COs in this pattern (see Special Techniques, page 162). When increasing or casting on sts, work increased sts in st pattern. When working across sts CO at beginning of row, it may be easier to work them in straight Stockinette stitch (St st) for the first row only, rather than Twisted St st.

Using larger circ needle, waste yarn and Provisional CO, CO 64 (66, 70, 72, 76, 78, 84) sts. (RS) Change to working yarn; begin Twisted St st. Work even until piece measures 6 ½ (6¾, 7 ½, 8, 8 ¼, 8 ¼, 8 ½)" from the beginning.

Shape Armholes (RS): Increase 1 st each side this row, then every other row 1 (1, 1, 2, 2, 3, 3) time(s), as

follows: K1-f/b, work to last st, k1-f/b–68 (70, 74, 78, 82, 86, 92) sts. Work even for 1 row.

Next Row (RS): CO 3 (4, 6, 7, 8, 10, 11) sts, work to end, CO 3 (4, 6, 7, 8, 10, 11) sts–74 (78, 86, 92, 98, 106, 114) sts. Work even for 1 row.

Next Row (RS): CO 5 (6, 8, 8, 9, 12, 13) sts, work to end, CO 5 (6, 8, 8, 9, 12, 13) sts–84 (90, 102, 108, 116, 130, 140) sts. Work even for 1 row. Transfer sts to waste yarn for Body.

FRONT

With RS facing, carefully unravel Provisional CO and place first and last 12 (12, 12, 14, 18, 20, 22) sts on larger circ needle for Fronts. Transfer remaining center 40 (42, 46, 44, 40, 38, 40) sts to waste yarn for Back neck. Place removable marker for top of shoulder. (RS) Working BOTH SIDES AT SAME TIME with separate balls of yarn, begin Twisted St st. Work even until piece measures same as for Back from top of shoulder to beginning of armhole shaping, ending with a WS row. Shape armholes as for Back, ending with a WS row–22 (24, 28, 32, 38, 46, 50) sts each Front. Break yarn for Right Front.

BODY

Join Back to Fronts (RS): With RS facing, transfer Back sts, then Right Front sts to left-hand end of needle. *Note: The Back sts referred to are the sts that were placed on waste yarn after working the armhole shaping, not the Back neck sts that were placed on waste yarn after unraveling the Provisional CO.* Your sts should now be in the following order, from right to left, with RS facing: Left Front, Back, Right Front. Using yarn attached to Left Front, work across Left Front, pm for left side, work across Back, pm for RS, work across Right Front–128 (138, 158, 172, 192, 222, 240) sts. Do NOT join. Working back and forth, work even for 1 row.

Shape Neck (RS): Increase 1 st each neck edge this row, every 4 rows 3 (2, 1, 1, 1, 6, 5) time(s), then every other row 9 (11, 13, 11, 12, 3, 6) times, as follows: K1-f/b, work to last st, k1-f/b–154 (166, 188, 198, 220, 242, 264) sts. Work even for 1 row.

Next Row (RS): CO 6 sts, work to end, CO 6 sts–166 (178, 200, 210, 232, 254, 276) sts.

Shape Waist (RS): Decrease 4 sts this row, then every 4 rows once, as follows: [Work to 3 sts before marker, ssk, k1-tbl, sm, k1-tbl, k2tog] twice–158 (170, 192, 202, 224, 246, 268) sts. Work even until piece measures 13 (13½, 14, 14½, 15, 15½, 16)" from top of shoulder, ending with a RS row, decrease 0 (0, 2, 0, 2, 0, 2) sts evenly on last row–158 (170, 190, 202, 222, 246, 266) sts remain. Work even for 1 row.

Next Row (RS): Change to smaller 32" long circ needle and 2×2 Rib. Work even for 3". BO all sts loosely knitwise.

FINISHING

Collar: With RS facing, using smaller 32" long circ needle, beginning above ribbing on Right Front, pick up and knit 6 sts in sts CO for Right Front neck, pm, pick up and knit 3 sts for every 4 rows to 1" below top of shoulder, pm, pick up and knit sts to top of shoulder, work across Back sts from waste yarn, pick up and knit sts for 1", pm, pick up and knit sts along Left Front to sts CO for Left Front neck, pm, pick up and knit 6 sts to edge. (WS) Knit 1 row. *Note: You will need a multiple of 4 sts + 2 to work the Collar ribbing. If you do not have the correct number of sts, you may increase or decrease sts on this first knit row to obtain the correct number. You should have the same number of sts along each Front. Begin 2×2 Rib, beginning with Row 2. Note: RS and WS rows are reversed here.*

Shape Collar

Note: Collar will be shaped using Short Rows (see Special Techniques, page 162). Hide wraps as you come to them.

Row 1 (RS): Work to last marker, sm, wrp-t.

Row 2: Repeat Row 1.

Row 3: Work to 3 sts after wrapped st of row before last row worked, wrp-t.

Repeat Row 3 until all sts have been worked. *Note: Depending on the number of sts you picked up, you may not end right at the last st. If you wish, on your last 2 rows, you may adjust the number of sts you work before working the wrap.*

Next Row (RS): Work across all sts, hiding remaining wrap as you come to it, and removing all markers. Work even until Collar measures 1 (1, 1½, 1½, 1½, 2, 2)" at lower edge, ending with a WS row. BO all sts loosely purlwise.

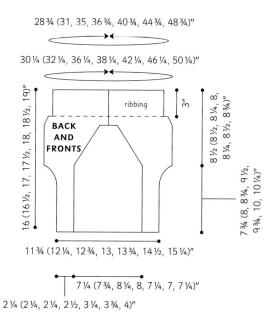

28¾ (31, 35, 36¾, 40¾, 44¾, 48¾)"

30¼ (32¼, 36¼, 38¼, 42¼, 46¼, 50¼)"

ribbing

3"

BACK AND FRONTS

16 (16½, 17, 17½, 18, 18½, 19)"

8½ (8½, 8¼, 8, 8¼, 8½, 8¾)"

7¾ (8, 8¾, 9½, 9¾, 10, 10¼)"

11¾ (12¼, 12¾, 13, 13¾, 14½, 15¼)"

7¼ (7¾, 8¼, 8, 7¼, 7, 7¼)"

2¼ (2¼, 2¼, 2½, 3¼, 3¾, 4)"

Armhole Edging: With RS facing, using 16" long circ needle, and beginning at bottom center of underarm, pick up and knit approximately 1 st for every st CO for the bottom of the armhole, and 3 sts for every 4 rows around the armhole, ending with a multiple of 4 sts. *Note: If you have a small gap at the armhole where the Back and Fronts were joined, you can close the gap when picking up the sts.* Join for working in the rnd; pm for beginning of rnd.

All Rnds: *K2, p2; repeat from * around. Work even until Edging measures ½". BO all sts loosely knitwise.

Place markers for 3 buttonholes along side edge of ribbing at bottom of Right Front, the first at top of ribbing, the last ½" from bottom edge, and the third evenly spaced between.

Note: You may work Overcast Button Loops (see page 96) instead of working the Crab Stitch Button Loop Edging.

Crab Stitch Button Loop Edging: With RS facing, using crochet hook, and beginning at BO edge of Right Front (beginning at neck edge for left-handed crocheters), work Crab St along side edge of ribbing.

Block as desired.

OVERCAST BUTTON LOOPS (optional)

Mark placement for beginning and ending point of each loop on edge of garment. To form core of loop, using tapestry needle and working yarn, *bring needle up at lower marker. Insert needle at upper marker. Pull yarn through, leaving a loop the desired size, preferably a little smaller than size of button. Repeat from * once. Work a buttonhole st over loop as follows: **Holding work in left hand, wrap yarn over left index finger from front to back, bring yarn through center of loop from back to front, then through strand on index finger from front to back, removing your finger from the strand. Slide resulting st down to base of loop, pulling it tight. Repeat from **, sliding each st down next to previous st worked, until entire loop is covered, making sure that buttonhole sts are closely packed next to each other. Fasten off on WS, secure end.

Sew buttons at markers, ½″ in from the edge. Block as desired.

MAKE IT YOUR OWN

For this variation, I created a pullover by working in the round instead of back-and-forth. To do this, work the pattern as written, but when the Front shaping is complete, work one wrong-side row, and at the end of the next right-side row, continue working across the left Front (join for working in the round at the same time), place a marker for the beginning of the round, and continue working in the round instead of flat. In order to keep the twisted stitch pattern correct, use your center Front marker as the beginning-of-round marker, and substitute plain knit rounds for the purl rounds called for in the stitch pattern. Proceed with the pattern and add an extra inch of ribbing. (This one has 4″ of ribbing.)

Once you have bound off the stitches at the end of the Body, make the cowl-neck collar by placing the reserved Back stitches on a spare needle. Pick up stitches as directed in the pattern with a smaller circular needle, but instead of working flat, place a marker and join for working in the round, continuing in knit 2, purl 2 rib. When the ribbing (measured from top Back neck to needles) is 3″, change to larger circular needle and work in pattern until the cowl neck measures 6 ½″. Bind off all stitches loosely knitwise.

Steam or block the garment. Turn the cowl neck under, and tack it down loosely to the inside of the neck edging.

This variation was worked in size Small, with 5 skeins of the same yarn used for the main version, but in color #5403. Read about estimating yarn requirements on page 160.

PARADISE BEACH COVER-UP

The Paradise Beach Cover-Up is worked a little differently than the other top-down set-in sleeve patterns in this book. Instead of casting on at the shoulder tops and working down to the underarm, this one is cast on and started at the center of the back and worked up toward the shoulders. To make the neckline, the center neck stitches are bound off, and on the next row, immediately cast back on. From there, you work down toward the underarm, join the garment in the round, and work down toward the bottom edge. Trying on as you go will assure a perfect fit and length. Wear it as a cover-up over a bathing suit or as a dress over a little silk slip.

SIZES

X-Small (Small/Medium, Large/
1X-Large, 2X-Large/3X-Large)

FINISHED MEASUREMENTS

33 (39, 45, 53)" chest

YARN

Gedifra Tiago (50% silk / 50%
viscose; 93 yards / 50 grams):
8 (9, 11, 12) balls #6804

NEEDLES

One 29" (74 cm) long or longer
circular (circ) needle size US 9
(5.5 mm)

One 29" (74 cm) long or longer
circ needle size US 10 (6 mm)

One or two 24" (60 cm) long or
longer circ needles or one set of
five double-pointed needles (dpn)
size US 10 (6 mm), as preferred,
for Sleeves

Change needle size if necessary
to obtain correct gauge.

NOTIONS

Removable marker; waste yarn;
stitch markers; assorted beads
with opening wide enough to fit
4 strands of yarn (optional)

GAUGE

16 sts and 18 rows = 4" (10 cm)
in 2×2 Rib, slightly stretched
width-wise, using smaller needle

YOKE BACK AND FRONT

Note: After the initial Provisional CO, use Backward Loop CO for any other COs in this pattern (see Special Techniques, page 162). When increasing or casting on sts, work increased sts in st pattern.

Using smaller circ needle, waste yarn and Provisional CO, CO 62 (70, 78, 82) sts. (RS) Change to working yarn; begin 2×2 Rib. Work even until piece measures 7 ½ (8 ½, 9, 9 ½)" from the beginning, ending with a WS row. Place removable marker at beginning of row to mark RS and top of shoulder.

Shape Neck (RS): Work 16 (18, 22, 24) sts, BO 30 (34, 34, 34) center sts loosely, work to end.

Next Row (WS): Work 16 (18, 22, 24) sts, CO 30 (34, 34, 34) sts, work to end. Work even until piece measures 7 ½ (8 ½, 9, 9 ½)" from top of shoulder, ending with a WS row.

PATTERN FEATURES
Top-down construction starting at mid-back, body worked in the round, provisional cast-on, short-repeat stitch pattern

ABBREVIATIONS

Sk2p2: Slip 1 st knitwise, k2, pass slipped st over 2 knit sts.

STITCH PATTERNS

2×2 Rib

(multiple of 4 sts + 2; 1-row repeat)
Row 1 (RS): K2, *p2, k2; repeat from * to end.
Row 2: Knit the knit sts and purl the purl sts as they face you.
Repeat Row 2 for 2×2 Rib.

Mesh Pattern

(multiple of 3 sts; 4-rnd repeat)
Rnd 1: *Yo, sk2p2; repeat from * to end.
Rnd 2: Knit.
Rnd 3: *Sk2p2, yo; repeat from * to end.
Rnd 4: Knit.
Repeat Rnds 1-4 for Mesh Pattern.

BODY

Join Back and Front

Shape Armholes (RS): With RS facing, carefully unravel Provisional CO and place Back sts on left-hand end of circ needle. Work across Front, CO 2 (4, 6, 12) sts for right underarm, place marker (pm) for right side, CO 2 (4, 6, 12) sts, work across Back, CO 2 (4, 6, 12) sts for left underarm, pm for beginning of rnd, CO 2 (4, 6, 12) sts, work to beginning of rnd marker—132 (156, 180, 212) sts. Work even until piece measures 11½ (13, 14½, 15½)" from top of shoulder, increase 0 (0, 0, 1) st on last rnd—132 (156, 180, 213) sts.

Next Rnd: Change to larger circ needle and Mesh Pattern. Work even until piece measures 25½ (26½, 27, 27½)" or 2" less than desired length from top of shoulder, ending with Rnd 2 or 4 of pattern, decrease 0 (0, 0, 1) sts evenly spaced on last rnd—132 (156, 180, 212) sts.

Next Rnd: Change to smaller needle and 2×2 Rib as follows: *K2, p2; repeat from * to end of rnd. Work even for 2". BO all sts loosely in pattern.

SLEEVES

Note: Use your preferred method of working in the rnd when working the Sleeves (see page 150).

With RS facing, using larger needle(s), beginning at bottom center of underarm, pick up and knit 63 (75, 84, 99) sts evenly around armhole. Join for working in the rnd; pm for beginning of rnd. Knit 1 rnd.

Next Rnd: Change to Mesh Pattern. Work even for 6", or to 2" less than desired length, ending with Rnd 2 or 4 of pattern, and increasing or decreasing sts on last rnd if necessary to end with a multiple of 4 sts.

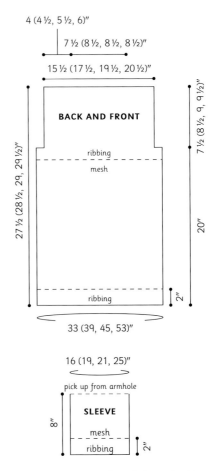

Note: Body is begun at center Back, worked over shoulders to center Front, then joined at armholes and worked down to bottom edge.

Next Rnd: *K2, p2; repeat from * around. Work even for 2″. BO all sts loosely in pattern.

FINISHING

Cord Tie: Cut 2 strands of yarn 6 times ribcage measurement (or at least 3 times desired finished length). With both strands held together, work Twisted Cord (see Special Techniques, page 162). Beginning and ending 1-2″ in from right side edge, thread Cord through Mesh just below ribbing. To add beads (optional), tie knot in both ends of Cord, leaving room between the knot and the end for the number of beads to be added, plus an extra 2″. Remove the original knot on the open end, and cut the Cord at the opposite end so that the Twisted strands unravel. Thread beads onto each end and secure with double knot after last bead. Trim ends if desired. Block as desired.

MAKE IT YOUR OWN

Once you have joined the Front and the Back, the empire waist can be adjusted simply by trying on as you go and stopping when you're happy with how it looks; just make sure to work the Front to the same length as the Back. And since the armholes have nice, clean edges that don't require finishing, you can skip the Sleeves altogether and have a sleeveless tunic fit for a Grecian goddess.

CHAPTER 4

Round-Yoke Sweaters

While round-yoke construction is typically applied to traditional ski sweaters (you know the ones with snowflakes around the top), I like to defy tradition and use it to create a broader array of style possibilities.

Round yokes are seamless and worked in the round (unless you are making a cardigan, which would be worked flat, but still in one piece). The yoke is shaped with decreases that are evenly distributed around the upper portion of the sweater. When making a round-yoke sweater with colorwork, it's best to work bottom up because it is easier to plan your motifs when working them as you decrease up toward the neck. (If you were to work a garment such as this top down, you'd have to make increases while doing colorwork at the same time, and if you use a lifted increase, you might reveal a bit of color from the row below it and mar your motif.) Trying on as you go in a bottom-up sweater construction is a little trickier because you'll be holding up the garment until it reaches your armpits—but it still works. If you are new to round yokes, check out Round-Yoke Cropped on page 104 to learn the basics.

ROUND-YOKE CROPPED

This classic cardigan is cast on at the hem and worked in rows to just under the arms. The sleeves are worked separately from wrist (or fingertip or elbow or wherever the heck you want your sleeve to fall) to armhole. Then, the whole thing is joined and worked in rows with a series of decreases leading up to the neckline, giving it the "round yoke" effect. Without seams to break up the flow, the variegated yarn shown becomes a constant swirl of color.

SIZES

X-Small (Small, Medium, Large, 1X-Large, 2X-Large, 3X-Large)

FINISHED MEASUREMENTS

30 (34, 38, 42, 46, 50, 54)" chest

YARN

Araucania Yarns Atacama (100% alpaca; 110 yards / 50 grams): 5 (6, 7, 8, 9, 11, 12) hanks #503

NEEDLES

One 29" (74 cm) long or longer circular (circ) needle size US 7 (4.5 mm)

One or two 24" (60 cm) long or longer circ needles or one set of five double-pointed needles (dpn) size US 7 (4.5 mm), as preferred, for Sleeves

One pair straight needles size US 7 (4.5 mm) (optional) for working Sleeves back and forth, if desired

Change needle size if necessary to obtain correct gauge.

NOTIONS

Stitch markers; waste yarn; removable markers; one 1" button

GAUGE

20 sts and 24 rows = 4" (10 cm) in Stockinette stitch (St st)

BODY

Using 29" circ needle, CO 150 (170, 190, 210, 230, 250, 270) sts. Working back and forth, begin Seed st. Work even for 1", ending with a WS row.

Next Row (RS): Work 7 sts in Seed st, place marker (pm), work in St st to last 7 sts, pm, work in Seed st to end. Work even until piece measures 8 (8½, 9, 10, 10, 10½, 11)" from the beginning, ending with a WS row.

Shape Armholes (RS): Work 31 (35, 40, 44, 48, 52, 57) sts, BO 12 (14, 14, 16, 18, 20, 20) sts for armhole, work 64 (72, 82, 90, 98, 106, 116) sts, BO 12 (14, 14, 16, 18, 20, 20) sts for underarm, work to end. *Note: If you prefer, you may transfer underarm sts to waste yarn for finishing later, instead of binding off (see Step 4, page 158).* Transfer sts and markers to waste yarn for Yoke. Break yarn.

SLEEVES

Note: Use your preferred method of working in the rnd when working the Sleeves (see page 150).

CO 34 (40, 44, 48, 52, 58, 62) sts. Join for working in the rnd, being careful not to twist sts; place marker (pm) for beginning of rnd. Begin Seed st. Work even for 1".

Next Rnd: Change to St st (knit every rnd). Work even for 6 rnds.

Shape Sleeve: Increase 2 sts this rnd, every 12 (10, 10, 8, 8, 8, 6) rnds 6 (5, 8, 9, 12, 9, 5) times, then every 0 (12,

---

PATTERN FEATURES

Bottom-up, round-yoke construction, sleeves worked in the round, short-row shaping

---

STITCH PATTERN

Seed Stitch

(multiple of 2 sts; 1-row/rnd repeat)

Row/Rnd 1 (RS): *K1, p1; repeat from * to end.

Row/Rnd 2: Purl the knit sts and knit the purl sts as they face you.

Repeat Row/Rnd 2 for Seed st.

0, 10, 0, 10, 8) rnds 0 (2, 0, 1, 0, 2, 8) times, as follows: K1, m1, work to last st, m1, k1—48 (56, 62, 70, 76, 82, 90) sts. Work even until piece measures 17¾ (18, 18¾, 19, 20, 20½, 20½)″ from the beginning, ending 6 (7, 7, 8, 9, 10, 10) sts before beginning of rnd on last rnd. BO 12 (14, 14, 16, 18, 20, 20) sts for underarm, work to end—36 (42, 48, 54, 58, 62, 70) sts remain. *Note: If you prefer, you may transfer underarm sts to waste yarn for finishing later, instead of binding off (see Step 4, page 158).* Transfer sts to waste yarn for Yoke. Break yarn.

YOKE

Join Body

With RS facing, transfer sts from waste yarn to 29″ long circ needle as follows: 31 (35, 40, 44, 48, 52, 57) sts for Left Front, 36 (42, 48, 54, 58, 62, 70) sts for Left Sleeve, 64 (72, 82, 90, 98, 106, 116) sts for Back, 36 (42, 48, 54, 58, 62, 70) sts for Right Sleeve, 31 (35, 40, 44, 48, 52, 57) sts for Right Front—198 (226, 258, 286, 310, 334, 370) sts.

Next Row (RS): Rejoin yarn to Right Front. Work 7 sts in Seed st, work in St st to last 7 sts, work in Seed st to end. Work even until Yoke measures 1½ (1½, 1½, 1½, 2, 2, 2½)″ from join, ending with a WS row.

Decrease Row 1 (RS): Work 7 sts in Seed st, k4 (2, 4, 2, 2, 1, 2), *k2tog, k3; repeat from * to last 12 (12, 12, 12, 11, 11, 11) sts, k2tog, k3 (3, 3, 3, 2, 2, 2), work in Seed st to end—162 (184, 210, 232, 251, 270, 299) sts remain. Work even until Yoke measures 3 (3, 3½, 3½, 4, 4, 4½)″ from join, decreasing 4 (3, 3, 3, 3, 3, 3) sts evenly spaced between Seed st borders on first row, and ending with a WS row—158 (181, 207, 229, 248, 267, 296) sts remain.

Decrease Row 2 (RS): Work 7 sts in Seed st, k1 (2, 1, 2, 2, 1, 2), *k2tog, k2; repeat from * to last 10 (12, 11, 12, 11, 11, 11) sts, k2tog, k1 (3, 2, 3, 2, 2, 2), work in Seed st to end—122 (140, 159, 176, 190, 204, 226) sts remain. Work even until Yoke measures 4½ (4½, 5½, 5½, 6, 6, 6½)″ from join, decreasing 4 sts evenly spaced between Seed st borders on first row, and ending with a WS row—118 (136, 155, 172, 186, 200, 222) sts remain.

Decrease Row 3 (RS): Work 7 sts in Seed st, k1 (1, 0, 1, 2, 3, 4), *k2tog, k1; repeat from * to last 11 (11, 10, 10, 12,

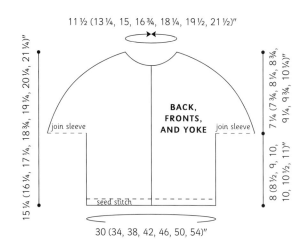

11½ (13¼, 15, 16¾, 18¼, 19½, 21½)″

15¼ (16¼, 17¼, 18¾, 19¼, 20¼, 21¼)″

BACK, FRONTS, AND YOKE

join sleeve

join sleeve

seed stitch

7¼ (7¾, 8¼, 8¾, 9¼, 9¾, 10¼)″

8 (8½, 9, 10, 10, 10½, 11)″

30 (34, 38, 42, 46, 50, 54)″

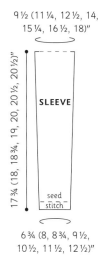

9½ (11¼, 12½, 14, 15¼, 16½, 18)″

SLEEVE

17¾ (18, 18¾, 19, 20, 20½, 20½)″

seed stitch

6¾ (8, 8¾, 9½, 10½, 11½, 12½)″

Note: Pieces are worked from the bottom up.

13, 13) sts, k2tog, k2 (2, 1, 2, 3, 4, 4), work in Seed st to end—84 (96, 108, 120, 130, 140, 155) sts remain. Work even until Yoke measures 6 (6 ½, 7, 7 ½, 8, 8 ½, 9)" from join, decreasing 2 (1, 0, 0, 0, 0, 0) sts evenly spaced between Seed st borders on first row, ending with a WS row 82 (95, 108, 120, 130, 140, 155) sts remain. Place removable marker 21 (24, 27, 30, 33, 35, 39) sts in from each edge.

Shape Back Neck

Note: Back neck will be shaped using Short Rows (see Special Techniques, page 162). Hide wraps as you come to them.

Next Row (RS): Work to 3 sts after second marker, wrp-t. Repeat last row 3 times.

Decrease Row 4 (RS): Hiding remaining wrap as you come to it, work 7 sts in Seed st, k1 (0, 1, 1, 1, 0, 0), *k2tog, k1; repeat from * to last 11 (10, 10, 10, 11, 10, 10) sts,

k2tog, k2 (1, 1, 1, 2, 1, 1), work in Seed st to end—60 (68, 77, 85, 92, 98, 108) sts remain. Work even for 1 row, decrease 3 (2, 2, 1, 1, 0, 0) sts evenly spaced between Seed st borders—57 (66, 75, 84, 91, 98, 108) sts remain.

Next Row: Change to Seed st across all sts. Work even for 2 rows.

Next Row (Buttonhole Row): Work 4 sts, yo, k2tog, work to end. Work even for 3 rows. BO all sts loosely in pattern.

FINISHING

Sew underarm seams. *Note: If you chose to transfer underarm sts to waste yarn instead of binding off, graft sts together using Kitchener stitch (see Special Techniques, page 162).* Sew button opposite buttonhole. Block as desired.

MAKE IT YOUR OWN

For this variation, I shortened and flared the Sleeves and widened the neckline. If you want to do the same, cast on an extra 2" worth of stitches for each Sleeve [that's a total of 58 (66, 72, 80, 86, 92, 100) stitches], then place a marker and join for working in the round. Work your Seed stitch edging, and do paired decreases (k1, k2tog, work to 3 sts before marker, ssk, k1) every sixth round a total of 5 times or until you have the final required number of stitches as in the original pattern. Then, when the Sleeve measures your desired length—probably 8 or 9", continue working it according to the pattern. And, if you want a shoulder-skimming neckline like the one here, work only Decrease Rows 1 and 2, work another inch, then skip the short-row shaping at the top Back. Work a Seed stitch border as instructed, or work an extra few rows for a more dramatic look. *Note: Try this on as you go. If your neckline is a bit too loose, you may opt to decrease an extra inch worth of stitches a row or two before you begin your neck edging.*

This variation was worked in size X-Small, with 6 skeins of Tahki / Stacy Charles Cotton Classic (100% mercerized cotton; 108 yards / 50 grams) in color #3533. Read about estimating yarn requirements on page 160.

SIZES

X-Small (Small, Medium, Large, 1X-Large, 2X-Large, 3X-Large)

FINISHED MEASUREMENTS

30½ (34½, 38½, 42½, 46½, 50½, 54½)″ chest

YARN

Elann Collection Peruvian Pure Alpaca (100% alpaca; 109 yards / 50 grams): 6 (7, 7, 8, 9, 10, 11) balls #786 plum heather (MC); 2 (2, 2, 3, 3, 3, 3) balls #791 Atlantic mist (A); 1 (1, 1, 1, 1, 2, 2) ball(s) #792 Atlantis (B); 1 ball #790 hyacinth (C)

NEEDLES

One 29″ (82 cm) long or longer circ needle size US 7 (4.5 mm)

One 29″ (82 cm) long or longer circular (circ) needle size US 6 (4 mm)

One or two 24″ (60 cm) long or longer circ needles or one set of five double-pointed needles (dpn) size US 7 (4.5 mm), as preferred, for Sleeves

Change needle size if necessary to obtain correct gauge.

NOTIONS

Stitch markers in 2 colors; waste yarn; sewing machine and coordinating thread; fourteen ⅛″ eyelets; eyelet pliers

GAUGE

20 sts and 26 rows = 4″ (10 cm) in Stockinette stitch (St st) using larger needles

UPDATED OLD CLASSIC

For me there's hardly anything more exciting than finding a way to spruce up an old classic. And that's what I've done here with the traditional round-yoke Fair Isle pullover.

It's now a tunic featuring waist shaping and belled sleeves and a dramatically deep V-neck that laces up with a twisted cord.

NOTES

This pullover is worked from the bottom up. The Body and Sleeves are worked separately in the round, then joined for the Yoke. The Body includes sts cast on for a neck steek, which will then be cut, creating neck facings which will be folded over and sewn to the WS.

BODY

With larger 29″ long circ needle and MC, CO 75 (85, 95, 105, 115, 125, 135) sts, place marker (pm) for side, CO 75 (85, 95, 105, 115, 125, 135) sts—150 (170, 190, 210, 230, 250, 270) sts. Join for working in the rnd, being careful not to twist sts; pm for beginning of rnd. Begin 1×1 Rib in-the-Round. Work even for 1″.

Next Rnd: Change to St st (knit every rnd). Work even until piece measures 3″ from the beginning.

Shape Waist

Set-Up Rnd: *Work 19 (21, 24, 26, 29, 31, 34) sts, place color B marker, work 37 (43, 47, 53, 57, 63, 67) sts, place color B marker*, work to next marker, slip marker (sm), repeat from * to * once, work to end.

Decrease Rnd: Decrease 4 sts this rnd, then every 6 rnds twice, as follows: [Work to 2 sts before next color B marker, k2tog, sm, work to next color B marker, sm, ssk] twice, work to end—138 (158, 178, 198, 218, 238, 258) sts remain. Work even until piece measures 6 (6½, 6½, 6½, 6½, 7, 7)″ from the beginning.

PATTERN FEATURES

Bottom-up, round-yoke construction, body and sleeves worked in the round, steeks, stranded colorwork, reading charts, short-row shaping (variation), application of metal eyelets, I-Cord

---

STITCH PATTERNS

1×1 Rib in-the-Round
(multiple of 2 sts; 1-rnd repeat)
All Rnds: *K1, p1; repeat from * around.

1×1 Rib
(multiple of 2 sts + 1; 1-row repeat)
Row 1 (WS): P1, *k1, p1; repeat from * to end.
Row 2: Knit the knit sts and purl the purl sts as they face you.
Repeat Row 2 for 1×1 Rib.

Increase Rnd: Increase 4 sts this rnd, then every 6 rnds twice, as follows: [Work to next color B marker, m1, sm, work to next color B marker, sm, m1] twice, work to end–150 (170, 190, 210, 230, 250, 270) sts. Work even for 1 rnd, removing all color B markers.

Next Rnd: K1, m1, work to next marker, k1, m1, work to end–152 (172, 192, 212, 232, 252, 272) sts. Work even for 4 rnds. *Note: If you prefer a shallower neck, work even to desired neck depth before working neck steek.*

Begin Neck Steek: Work 38 (43, 48, 53, 58, 63, 68) sts, pm, CO 7 sts for neck steek, pm, work to end–159 (179, 199, 219, 239, 259, 279) sts. Work even until piece measures 14½" from the beginning, knitting across 7 steek sts on all rnds, and ending 6 (6, 7, 8, 9, 10, 10) sts before end of last rnd.

Shape Armholes: BO 12 (12, 14, 16, 18, 20, 20) sts for left underarm, removing marker, work to 6 (6, 7, 8, 9, 10, 10) sts before next marker, BO 12 (12, 14, 16, 18, 20, 20) sts for right underarm, removing marker, work to end. *Note: If you prefer, you may transfer underarm sts to waste yarn for finishing later, instead of binding off (see Step 4, page 158). Set aside, but do not break yarn.*

SLEEVES

Note: Sleeves are worked in the rnd from the cuff up. Use your preferred method of working in the rnd when working the Sleeves (see page 150).

With larger needle(s) and MC, CO 50 (52, 56, 58, 60, 62, 68) sts. Join for working in the rnd, being careful not to twist sts; pm for beginning of rnd. Begin 1×1 Rib in-the-Round. Work even for 1".

Next Rnd: Change to St st. Work even until piece measures 3" from the beginning.

Shape Sleeve

Decrease Rnd: Decrease 2 sts this rnd, then every 6 (5, 6, 5, 5, 4, 4) rnds 5 (6, 6, 7, 7, 9, 9) times, as follows: K1, k2tog, work to last 3 sts, ssk, k1–38 (38, 42, 42, 44, 42, 48) sts remain. Work even until piece measures 8½ (8½, 9, 9, 9, 10, 10)" from the beginning.

Increase Rnd: Increase 2 sts this rnd, then every 6 (6, 6, 5, 4, 3, 3) rnds 5 (6, 7, 10, 12, 17, 17) times, as follows: K1, m1, work to last st, m1, k1–50 (52, 58, 64, 70, 78, 84) sts. Work even until piece measures 17¾ (18, 18¾, 19, 20, 20½, 20½)" from the beginning, ending 6 (6, 7, 8, 9, 10, 10) sts before end of last rnd.

Shape Armholes: BO 12 (12, 14, 16, 18, 20, 20) sts for underarm, work to end–38 (40, 44, 48, 52, 58, 64) sts remain. *Note: If you prefer, you may transfer underarm sts to waste yarn for finishing later, instead of binding off (see Step 4, page 158). Break yarn and set aside.*

YOKE

With yarn attached to Body, k38 (40, 44, 48, 52, 58, 64) Left Sleeve sts, k71 (81, 89, 97, 105, 113, 123) Front sts, slipping steek markers, k38 (40, 44, 48, 52, 58, 64) Right Sleeve sts, k64 (74, 82, 90, 98, 106, 116) Back sts–211 (235, 259, 283, 307, 335, 367) sts. Join for working in the rnd; work to second steek marker, which is now new beginning of rnd marker. Work even for 11 (13, 15, 16, 19, 21, 22) rnds.

Begin Charts

Next Rnd: Work Chart A to first steek marker, changing colors as indicated, sm, k1 in MC, [k1 in A, k1 in MC] 3 times. Work even until 2 vertical repeats of Chart A are complete.

Next Rnd: Change to A. Work even for 0 (1, 2, 4, 4, 5, 5) rnds.

Shape Yoke

Decrease Rnd 1: *K2, k2tog; repeat from * to first steek marker, knit to end–160 (178, 196, 214, 232, 253, 277) sts remain.

Next Rnd: Mark center Back st [you may be off-center by 1 st]. This will be st 7 of Chart B. Counting from center

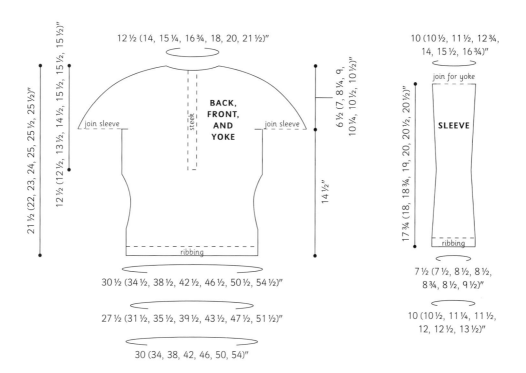

12 ½ (14, 15 ¼, 16 ¾, 18, 20, 21 ½)"

21 ½ (22, 23, 24, 25, 25 ½, 25 ½)"

12 ½ (12 ½, 13 ½, 14 ½, 15 ½, 15 ½, 15 ½)"

join sleeve

BACK, FRONT, AND YOKE

steek

join sleeve

6 ½ (7, 8 ¼, 9, 10 ¼, 10 ½, 10 ½)"

14 ½"

ribbing

30 ½ (34 ½, 38 ½, 42 ½, 46 ½, 50 ½, 54 ½)"

27 ½ (31 ½, 35 ½, 39 ½, 43 ½, 47 ½, 51 ½)"

30 (34, 38, 42, 46, 50, 54)"

10 (10 ½, 11 ½, 12 ¾, 14, 15 ½, 16 ¾)"

join for yoke

SLEEVE

17 ¾ (18, 18 ¾, 19, 20, 20 ½, 20 ½)"

ribbing

7 ½ (7 ½, 8 ½, 8 ½, 8 ¾, 8 ½, 9 ½)"

10 (10 ½, 11 ¼, 11 ½, 12, 12 ½, 13 ½)"

Back st, around right shoulder to beginning of rnd marker, determine where you must start Chart B at beginning of rnd in order to end with st 7 on center Back st. *Note: You will likely have an incomplete repeat of the snowflake motif on either side of the steek sts.* Change to Chart B, beginning with st as determined, work to steek marker, sm, k1 in A, [k1 in B, k1 in A] 3 times. Work even until Chart B is complete. *Note: When working Row 7 of Chart B, work across steek sts as follows: K1 in C, [k1 in B, k1 in C] 3 times.*

Decrease Rnd 2: Change to A. *K1, k2tog; repeat from * to first steek marker, knit to end—109 (121, 133, 145, 157, 171, 187) sts remain.

Next Rnd: Work Chart A to first steek marker, changing colors as indicated, sm, k1 in MC, [k1 in A, k1 in MC] 3 times. *Note: You will have an incomplete repeat at the end of the rnd.* Work even until 1 (1, 1, 2, 2, 2, 2) vertical repeats of Chart A are complete. Work even for 0 (1, 2, 4, 4, 5, 5) rnds.

Decrease Rnd 3: Change to A. K1 (2, 0, 1, 0, 2, 0), *k1, [k2tog] twice; repeat from * to last 8 (9, 8, 9, 7, 9, 7) sts, knit to end, slipping steek marker—69 (77, 83, 91, 97, 107, 115) sts remain.

Next Rnd: Change to MC. Work even for 3 (2, 5, 2, 6, 5, 3) rnds. BO all sts loosely.

FINISHING

Sew underarm seams. *Note: If you chose to transfer underarm sts to waste yarn instead of binding off, graft sts together using Kitchener stitch (see Special Techniques, page 162).*

Neck Steek

Using sewing machine, with small st and relatively loose tension, sew a line from top of steek to bottom, just next to the center st of the steek, being careful to include the CO edge, but not to sew into the sts below the CO edge. Work a second line on the opposite side of the center st. If desired, you may reinforce the steek further by sewing an additional line to the outside of each of the existing lines. Being careful not to cut the machine stitching, create facings by cutting the center column of sts between the machine stitching, from BO edge to CO edge of steek. Fold facings and tack to WS, being careful not to let sts show on RS.

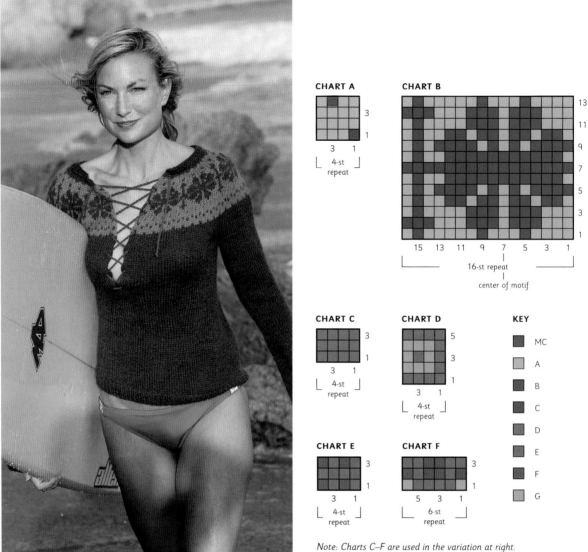

CHART A

3

1

3　　1
└ 4-st ┘
repeat

CHART B

13

11

9

7

5

3

1

15　13　11　9　7　5　3　1

└──── 16-st repeat ────┘
│
center of motif

CHART C

3

1

3　　1
└ 4-st ┘
repeat

CHART D

5

3

1

3　　1
└ 4-st ┘
repeat

KEY

■ MC

□ A

■ B

■ C

■ D

■ E

■ F

■ G

CHART E

3

1

3　　1
└ 4-st ┘
repeat

CHART F

3

1

5　3　1
└ 6-st ┘
repeat

Note: Charts C–F are used in the variation at right.

Neckband: With RS facing, using MC and smaller circ needle, beginning at top of neck opening, pick up and knit approximately 1 st for every BO st around neck edge, ending with an odd number of sts. Begin 1×1 Rib. Work even for 3 rows. BO all sts loosely in pattern.

Neck Eyelets: Using eyelets and eyelet pliers, insert eyelets in pairs (one eyelet on each side of neck opening), with first pair of eyelets at base of steek, last pair just below ribbing, and remaining pairs evenly spaced between. *Note: Do NOT punch through the strands of yarn as this may cause the sts to unravel. Instead, work each eyelet carefully into the V of a st, or between sts, before setting the eyelet with the pliers.*

Twisted Cord: Cut 2 strands of C 4 yards long. Work Twisted Cord (see Special Techniques, page 162). Tie overhand knot in both ends. Beginning at bottom of neck opening, thread Cord through eyelets as you would for a shoe.

Block as desired.

MAKE IT YOUR OWN

Make a short-sleeve version like this one as follows: Work the Body to the underarm. Using smaller needles, cast on the same number of stitches that are required for the long sleeves after all shaping is completed—50 (56, 62, 68, 74, 80, 82) stitches. Join for working in the round and work in knit 1, purl 1 rib for 1". Change to larger needles and knit all rounds until the Sleeve is the desired length to your underarm. Beginning on the next round, bind off the underarm stitches as the pattern directs, and continue with the directions, as written, from that point forward.

For a more modest neckline, cast on for the steek just after the Body and Sleeves are joined (instead of just after the waist shaping is completed).

You can also add short-row shaping (see Special Techniques, page 162) to the Back, just after your last decrease round, to lift the Back of the sweater for a closer fit. To add short-row shaping, place removable markers where the top point of your shoulders would be if you were wearing the sweater. *Note: Hide all wraps as you come to them.*

Rows 1 (RS) and 2: Working back and forth in St st, work to 3 sts after second marker, slip marker (sm), wrp-t.

Row 3: Work to 3 sts after wrapped st of row before last row worked, wrp-t.

Repeat Row 3 three times. Work to the end, and continue working the Yoke for the number of rounds specified in the pattern, hiding the last wrap on the first round as you come to it. Complete the pattern as written.

This variation was worked in size Small and has a Yoke depth of 7½". The Yoke Charts were worked in the following order, with 1 or 2 plain knit rows in between them: C, D, E, F, C. I used Nashua Handknits Creative Focus Worsted (75% wool / 25% alpaca; 220 yards / 100 grams): 3 balls of #4899 khaki (E), and less than 1 ball each of #2190 copper (D), #3686 Carolina blue (G), and #1092 zinnia (F). Read about estimating yarn requirements on page 160.

CHAPTER 5

Designing on the Fly

When you design on the fly, you're knitting in a
no-rules zone. It's fun because if you know what your
stitch and row gauge are, you can make a garment—
probably the simpler the better to begin with—
without following much of a pattern at all. In fact,
all you need are a simple set of principles, a vision,
and possibly a stitch dictionary. I designed all
of the projects in this chapter on the fly and am
hoping that what you see here will inspire you to
spread your designer wings.

FAB WRAP

I had a vision in my head of how I wanted this wrap to fit, and to make it reality I used a standard bath towel as a prototype. I simply wrapped the towel around my shoulders, then folded and pinned until it fit me "just so," then made note of the dimensions. (Just don't tell anyone that I used a towel my mother-in-law swiped from a Las Vegas hotel room a couple of years ago.)

FINISHED MEASUREMENTS
Approximately 35" wide x 22" long, slightly stretched

YARN
Misti Alpaca Chunky (100% alpaca; 108 yards / 100 grams): 3 hanks #623 ember mélange

NEEDLES
One 29" (74 cm) long circular (circ) needle size US 11 (8 mm)
Change needle size if necessary to obtain correct gauge.

NOTIONS
One 1" button or brooch (optional)

GAUGE
12 sts and 20 rows = 4" (10 cm) in pattern, slightly stretched

CO 105 sts.

Establish Pattern

Row 1 (RS): K5, *p3, k2; repeat from * to last 5 sts, k5.

Row 2: K5, *p2, k3; repeat from * to last 5 sts, k5.

Work even until piece measures 22" from the beginning. BO all sts loosely in pattern.

Fold wrap in half lengthwise so that WSs are together, allowing about 1" of CO edge to show. Tack the halves together in at least three places so it won't unfold as you wear it.

Either place a button about 15 sts in from the side edge, just below the fold, and push it through the stitches to close the wrap, or use a brooch (or three) as a closure and be extra fab.

MAKE IT YOUR OWN

Find a piece of fabric or a towel and drape it or fold it until you have a shape and size that'll mimic how you want your finished wrap to look. Make note of the length and width measurements.

The math is easy: Once you decide how wide you want it to be, do a gauge swatch in your chosen stitch pattern, find out how many stitches you get per inch, and multiply that number by the desired number of inches in width. Conversely, if you want to work your own Fab Wrap lengthwise, multiply the number of inches in length you want your completed wrap to be by the number of stitches per inch, and cast on that number. In either case, make sure that you have enough stitches to work full repeats of your chosen stitch pattern; you may also want to add edge stitches on either side if the piece needs a more finished edge, or one that won't roll. Work in pattern to your desired length or width, and bind off.

LOOKS GOOD ON ALL SIDES SCARF AND WRAP

I like scarves and wraps that look good on both sides. We all know that Garter stitch looks the same on both sides, but I think Garter stitch is kind of bleh, and I don't think we need any more bleh if we can avoid it. So, with this in mind, I scoured all the stitch dictionaries I could get my hands on and then chose the Moss Diamond and Lozenge pattern from *A Second Treasury of Knitting Patterns* for the scarf, and the Chevron pattern from *A Treasury of Knitting Patterns* for the wrap on page 120 (both books by Barbara G. Walker).

SCARF (see left)
CO 46 sts.

All Rows: Work 5 sts in Seed st, place marker (pm), work in Moss Diamond and Lozenge Pattern to last 5 sts, pm, work 5 sts in Seed st. Work even, keeping first and last 5 sts of every row in Seed st, until piece measures approximately 55" from the beginning, ending with Row 2 or 24 of Moss Diamond and Lozenge Pattern. BO all sts loosely in pattern.

FINISHING
Block to measurements.

WRAP (see page 120)
CO 79 sts.

All Rows: K3, place marker (pm), work in Chevron Pattern to last 3 sts, pm, k3. Work even, keeping first and last 3 sts of every row in Garter st (knit every row), until piece measures approximately 70" from the beginning, ending with Row 16 of Chevron Pattern. BO all sts loosely in pattern.

FINISHING
Block to measurements.

PATTERN FEATURES
Long-repeat stitch pattern

FINISHED MEASUREMENTS

Scarf: 9" wide x 55" long, before blocking

Wrap: 16" wide x 70" long, before blocking

YARN

Scarf: Karabella Yarns Empire Silk (100% silk; 90 yards / 50 grams): 5 balls #509

Wrap: Tahki Yarns Cotton Classic (100% mercerized cotton; 108 yards / 50 grams): 8 hanks #3913

NEEDLES

Scarf: One pair straight needles size US 7 (4.5 mm)

Wrap: One pair straight needles size US 6 (4 mm)

Change needle size if necessary to obtain correct gauge.

NOTIONS

Stitch markers

GAUGE

Scarf: 18 sts and 24 rows = 4" (10 cm) in Stockinette stitch (St st)

Wrap: 20 sts and 26 rows = 4" (10 cm) in Chevron Pattern

STITCH PATTERNS

Seed Stitch
(multiple of 2 sts + 1; 1-row repeat)
All Rows: K1, *p1, k1; repeat from * to end.

Moss Diamond and Lozenge Pattern
(for Scarf shown on page 118)
(multiple of 12 sts; 44-row repeat)
Rows 1 and 2: *K6, p6; repeat from * to end.
Rows 3 and 4: *P1, k5, p5, k1; repeat from * to end.
Rows 5 and 6: *K1, p1, k4, p4, k1, p1; repeat from * to end.
Rows 7 and 8: *P1, k1, p1, k3, p3, k1, p1, k1; repeat from * to end.
Rows 9 and 10: *[K1, p1] twice, k2, p2, [k1, p1] twice; repeat from * to end.
Rows 11 and 12: *P1, k1; repeat from * to end.
Rows 13 and 14: *K1, p1; repeat from * to end.
Rows 15 and 16: *[P1, k1] twice, p2, k2, [p1, k1] twice; repeat from * to end.
Rows 17 and 18: *K1, p1, k1, p3, k3, p1, k1, p1; repeat from * to end.
Rows 19 and 20: *P1, k1, p4, k4, p1, k1; repeat from * to end.
Rows 21 and 22: *K1, p5, k5, p1; repeat from * to end.
Rows 23 and 24: *P6, k6; repeat from * to end.
Rows 25 and 26: *P5, k1, p1, k5; repeat from * to end.
Rows 27 and 28: *P4, [k1, p1] twice, k4; repeat from * to end.
Rows 29 and 30: *P3, [k1, p1] 3 times, k3; repeat from * to end.
Rows 31 and 32: *P2, [k1, p1] 4 times, k2; repeat from * to end.
Rows 33-36: Repeat Rows 11-14.
Rows 37 and 38: *K2, [p1, k1] 4 times, p2; repeat from * to end.
Rows 39 and 40: *K3, [p1, k1] 3 times, p3; repeat from * to end.
Rows 41 and 42: *K4, [p1, k1] twice, p4; repeat from * to end.
Rows 43 and 44: *K5, p1, k1, p5; repeat from * to end.
Repeat Rows 1-44 for Moss Diamond and Lozenge Pattern.

Chevron Pattern

(for Wrap shown at left)

(multiple of 8 sts + 1; 16-row repeat)

Row 1: K1, *p7, k1; repeat from * to end.

Row 2: P1, *k7, p1; repeat from * to end.

Row 3: K2, *p5, k3; repeat from * to last 7 sts, p5, k2.

Row 4: P2, *k5, p3; repeat from * to last 7 sts, k5, p2.

Row 5: K3, *p3, k5; repeat from * to last 6 sts, p3, k3.

Row 6: P3, *k3, p5; repeat from * to last 6 sts, k3, p3.

Row 7: K4, *p1, k7; repeat from * to last 5 sts, p1, k4.

Row 8: P4, *k1, p7; repeat from * to last 5 sts, k1, p4.

Row 9: Repeat Row 2.

Row 10: Repeat Row 1.

Row 11: Repeat Row 4.

Row 12: Repeat Row 3.

Row 13: Repeat Row 6.

Row 14: Repeat Row 5.

Row 15: Repeat Row 8.

Row 16: Repeat Row 7.

Repeat Rows 1-16 for Chevron Pattern.

MAKE IT YOUR OWN

There are loads of stitch dictionaries out there and they are a great place to start if you want to design your own scarf or wrap. To start, find some stitch patterns you like. Work up a couple of swatches in a selection of yarns; make your swatches large enough so you can really see how the patterns look and how the yarn drapes. Decide which pattern you like best, and take into consideration whether or not you can actually see the pattern with the selected yarn.

To find out how many stitches you'll need to cast on, measure your gauge, decide how wide you want your wrap to be, and multiply your finished width by the number of stitches per inch you got with your gauge. Make sure that you have enough stitches to be able to work full repeats of your chosen stitch pattern. Then, add a few or more stitches, such as Garter stitch or Seed stitch, to either side of the wrap for some sort of border—otherwise the edges of your scarf or wrap might roll.

SIZES

X-Small (Small, Medium, Large,
1X-Large, 2X-Large, 3X-Large)

FINISHED MEASUREMENTS

30 (32, 34, 36, 38, 40, 44)" chest

YARN

Knit One Crochet Too Ambrosia
(70% baby alpaca / 20% silk /
10% cashmere; 137 yards / 50
grams): 4 (5, 5, 6, 6, 7, 7) balls
#146 ivory

NEEDLES

One 29" (74 cm) long or longer
circular (circ) needle size US 3
(3.25 mm)

One 29" (74 cm) long or longer
circ needle size US 4 (3.5 mm)

One 16" (40 cm) long circ needle
size US 3 (3.25 mm)

Change needle size if necessary
to obtain correct gauge.

NOTIONS

Stitch markers; waste yarn

GAUGE

24 sts and 30 rows = 4" (10 cm)
in Stockinette stitch (St st) using
larger needles

ESSENTIAL TANK

Anyone who knows anything knows that those men's tanks you can buy in
packages of three at your local department store are simply fabulous.
There's something about the cut—if you buy the right size, they fit well
and they aren't too short, either. Problem is, you can't really wear them
out and about unless you want to be known as someone who wears men's
underwear in public.

So I got to thinking. Why can't we knit a version in, say, cashmere,
or maybe alpaca? Why can't we also call it a semi-quick knit? And let the
bottom of the tank roll a bit? Why can't we put some teeny tiny ribs up
the center of the front for a little bit of sass?

We can . . . you can . . . and, heck, anyone who knows how to knit,
purl, and do a few increases or decreases can, too. This one is worked
from the bottom up and in the round. Why? This is a tank with strap-
like fronts, and if we were to work from the top down, it wouldn't
be as straightforward as starting out in one piece with the widest
circumference. (Remember, knitting on the fly has no rules!)

PATTERN FEATURES
Bottom-up construction, body worked in the round

STITCH PATTERN

2×2 Rib
(panel of 18 sts; 1-rnd repeat)
All Rnds: P2, [k2, p2] 8 times.

NOTES

This Tank is worked in the round to the armholes, then the Front and Back are worked separately. The tops of the Straps are grafted together to avoid seams. The bottom hem and neck and armhole edgings are worked so that the edges roll slightly.

BODY

With smaller 29″ long circ needle, CO 90 (96, 102, 108, 114, 120, 132) sts for Front, place marker (pm) for side, CO 90 (96, 102, 108, 114, 120, 132) sts for Back—180 (192, 204, 216, 228, 240, 264) sts. Join for working in the rnd, being careful not to twist sts; pm for beginning of rnd. Begin St st (knit every rnd). Work even for 5 rnds. Purl 1 rnd. *Note: This will create a ridge that will help control the hem roll; or it will allow you to turn the bottom under if you prefer to hem the garment later.*

Begin Pattern: Change to larger circ needle. K36 (39, 42, 45, 48, 51, 57), pm, work 18 sts in 2×2 Rib, pm, knit to end. Work even until piece measures 4¾ (4¾, 5¼, 5¼, 5¼, 5¾, 5¾)″ from the beginning.

Shape Waist

Decrease Rnd: Decrease 4 sts this rnd, then every 9 rnds twice, as follows: K1, k2tog, work to 3 sts before next marker, ssk, k1, slip marker (sm), k1, k2tog, work to last 3 sts, ssk, k1—168 (180, 192, 204, 216, 228, 252) sts remain. Work even until piece measures 9¾ (9¾, 10¼, 10¾, 11¼, 11¾, 12¾)″ from the beginning.

Increase Rnd: Increase 4 sts this rnd, then every 9 rnds twice, as follows: K1, m1, work to 1 st before next marker, m1, k1, slip marker (sm), k1, m1, work to last st, m1, k1—180 (192, 204, 216, 228, 240, 264) sts. Work even until piece measures 13¾ (14¼, 14¾, 14¾, 15¼, 15¾, 15¾)″ from the beginning.

FRONT

Shape Armholes: BO 8 (9, 10, 11, 11, 11, 13) sts, work to next marker. Transfer next 90 (96, 102, 108, 114, 120, 132) sts to waste yarn for Back—82 (87, 92, 97, 103, 109, 119) sts remain.

Next Row (WS): Working back and forth, BO 8 (9, 10, 11, 11, 11, 13) sts, work to end—74 (78, 82, 86, 92, 98, 106) sts remain.

Decrease Row 1 (RS): K1, k2tog, work to last 3 sts, k2tog-tbl, k1—72 (76, 80, 84, 90, 96, 104) sts remain.

Decrease Row 2 (WS): P1, p2tog-tbl, work to last 3 sts, p2tog, p1—70 (74, 78, 82, 88, 94, 102) sts remain.

Repeat last 2 rows 2 (2, 3, 3, 3, 4, 5) times—62 (66, 66, 70, 76, 78, 82) sts remain. Repeat Decrease Row 1 every other row 4 (5, 4, 6, 6, 6, 6) times—54 (56, 58, 58, 64, 66, 70) sts remain. Work even until armhole measures 5 (5½, 6, 6½, 6½, 7, 7)″, ending with a WS row.

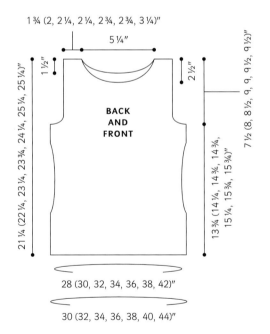

1¾ (2, 2¼, 2¼, 2¾, 2¾, 3¼)″

5¼″

1½″

2½″

7½ (8, 8½, 9, 9, 9½, 9½)″

21¼ (22¼, 23¼, 23¾, 24¼, 25¼, 25¼)″

BACK AND FRONT

13¾ (14¼, 14¾, 14¾, 15¼, 15¾, 15¾)″

28 (30, 32, 34, 36, 38, 42)″

30 (32, 34, 36, 38, 40, 44)″

Shape Neck (RS): Work 17 (18, 19, 19, 22, 23, 25) sts, join a second ball of yarn, BO center 20 sts, work to end. Working BOTH SIDES AT SAME TIME, BO 2 sts each neck edge once, then decrease 1 st each neck edge every row 4 times—11 (12, 13, 13, 16, 17, 19) sts remain each side for shoulders. Work even until armhole measures 7 ½ (8, 8 ½, 9, 9, 9 ½, 9 ½)", ending with a WS row. Break yarn. Transfer sts to waste yarn for finishing.

BACK

Transfer sts from waste yarn to larger circ needle. *Note: These are the sts that were placed on waste yarn after beginning the armhole shaping for the Front.*

Shape Armholes (RS): Rejoin yarn, BO 8 (9, 10, 11, 11, 11, 13) sts at beginning of next 2 rows, then complete armhole shaping as for Front—54 (56, 58, 58, 64, 66, 70) sts remain. Work even until armhole measures 6 (6 ½, 7, 7 ½, 7 ½, 8, 8)", ending with a WS row. Complete as for Front, from beginning of neck shaping.

Using Kitchener St (see Special Techniques, page 162), graft Front and Back shoulders together. *Note: If you prefer, you may graft them together using Three-Needle BO (see Special Techniques, page 162). Grafting them together will give a flatter shoulder seam.*

FINISHING

Weave in all ends.

Armhole Edging: With RS facing, using 16" long circ needle, beginning at bottom center of underarm, pick up and knit approximately 1 st for every BO st and 1 st for every 1 or 2 rows around the armhole. Join for working in the rnd; pm for beginning of rnd. Knit 2 rnds. BO all sts loosely.

Neck Edging: With RS facing, using 16" long circ needle, beginning at center Back neck, pick up and knit 1 st for every BO st and 1 st for every 1 or 2 rows around the neckline. Work as for armhole edging.

Hem: The hem of this Tank was designed to roll. Some yarns will roll uncontrollably, even after blocking. If this is the case, and you would prefer a finished hem, simply turn the bottom under at the purl rnd and loosely sew to WS, being careful not to let sts show on RS.

Block as desired.

MAKE IT YOUR OWN

There wasn't any voodoo involved here, so if you have a favorite tank, you can copy it, too, as long as it has simple lines. Here's how: Make a gauge swatch with your chosen yarn. Then take measurements of your favorite tank top and cast on a number of stitches to equal the circumference at the bottom edge. When working from the bottom edge up toward the shoulders, it helps to occasionally lay your knitting on top of the tank to check your progress. I added a tiny bit of shaping so it wasn't too boxy, but basically copied the lines of the garment. The armholes and the neckline are a bit trickier to improvise—refer to the shaping in this pattern for a little guidance. This isn't a true beginner project, but if you have a little moxie, or are just plain desperate to copy your favorite tank, it's likely you'll end up with a true original.

SIZES

X-Small (Small, Medium Large,
1X-Large, 2X-Large, 3X-Large)

FINISHED MEASUREMENTS

30 (34½, 39, 43¼, 46, 49½,
52¼)" chest, including bands

YARN

Artyarns Supermerino (100%
merino wool; 104 yards / 50
grams): 6 (7, 8, 9, 9, 10, 11)
hanks #246

NEEDLES

One 32" (82 cm) long or longer
circular (circ) needle size US 7
(4.5 mm)

One or two 24" (60 cm) long or
longer circ needles or one set of
five double-pointed needles (dpn)
size US 7 (4.5 mm), as preferred,
for Sleeves

Change needle size if necessary
to obtain correct gauge.

NOTIONS

Stitch markers; cable needle
(cn); waste yarn; 7 (7, 7, 8, 8, 8,
8) 1⅛" buttons

GAUGE

18 sts and 26 rows = 4" (10 cm)
in Stockinette stitch (St st)

FAVORITE CARDIGAN

I have a favorite cardigan. And the thing is, it's not even that well made.
In fact, it's literally falling apart. Worse, I bought it on a whim a few years
ago for nineteen bucks at a discount store and now there's no way I'd be
able to find another one just like it.

So, I got to thinking. Why not design a similar sweater and make
improvements on the old one? I know I could never copy it exactly, nor
would I want to: It has teeny tiny machine-knit stitches and it'd probably
take me thirty years to hand-knit such a thing. But my version has a
similar shape and feel. It's a raglan knitted from the top down to the
bottom edge.

PATTERN FEATURES
Top-down construction, sleeves worked in the round, cables

ABBREVIATIONS

C6B: Slip next 3 sts to cn, hold to back, k3, k3 from cn.

STITCH PATTERNS

2×2 Rib
(multiple of 4 sts + 2; 1-row repeat)
Row 1 (WS): P2, *k2, p2; repeat from * to end.
Row 2: Knit the knit sts and purl the purl sts as they face you.
Repeat Row 2 for 2×2 Rib.

2×2 Rib in-the-Round
(multiple of 4 sts; 1-rnd repeat)
All Rnds: *K2, p2; repeat from * around.

Cable Pattern
(panel of 10 sts; 6-row/rnd repeat)
Row/Rnd 1 (RS): P2, k6, p2.
Rows/Rnds 2-4: Knit the knit sts and purl the purl sts as they face you.
Row/Rnd 5: P2, C6B, p2.
Row/Rnd 6: Repeat Row/Rnd 2.
Repeat Rows/Rnds 1-6 for Cable Pattern.

NOTE

This Cardigan is designed to sit off the shoulders.

YOKE

With 32″ long circ needle, CO 106 (110, 118, 122, 130, 130, 134) sts. Begin 2×2 Rib. Do NOT join. Work even until piece measures 2″ from the beginning, ending with a WS row.

Begin Pattern (RS): Work 4 sts in 2×2 Rib, 10 sts in Cable Pattern, 3 (3, 5, 5, 6, 6, 7) sts in St st, place marker (pm) for Left Front, work 5 (6, 6, 7, 8, 8, 8) sts in St st, 10 sts in Cable Pattern, 5 (6, 6, 7, 8, 8, 8) sts in St st, pm for Left Sleeve, work 32 (32, 36, 36, 38, 38, 40) sts in St st, pm for Back, work 5 (6, 6, 7, 8, 8, 8) sts in St st, 10 sts in Cable Pattern, 5 (6, 6, 7, 8, 8, 8) sts in St st, pm for Right Sleeve, work 3 (3, 5, 5, 6, 6, 7) sts in St st, 10 sts in Cable Pattern, work in 2×2 Rib to end. Work even for 1 row.

Shape Raglan (RS): Increase 8 sts this row, then every other row 13 (17, 18, 21, 22, 23, 26) times, as follows: [Work to 1 st before next marker, k1-f/b, slip marker (sm), k1-f/b] 4 times, work to end—218 (254, 270, 298, 314, 322, 350) sts [31 (35, 38, 41, 43, 44, 48) sts each Front; 48 (58, 60, 68, 72, 74, 80) sts each Sleeve; 60 (68, 74, 80, 84, 86, 94) sts for Back].

BODY

Next Row (RS): Work to first marker, transfer next 48 (58, 60, 68, 72, 74, 80) sts to waste yarn for Right Sleeve, removing markers, CO 1 (2, 4, 6, 7, 10, 9) sts for underarm, pm for side, CO 1 (2, 4, 6, 7, 10, 9) sts for underarm, work to next marker, transfer next 48 (58, 60, 68, 72, 74, 80) sts to waste yarn for Left Sleeve, removing markers, CO 1 (2, 4, 6, 7, 10, 9) sts for underarm, pm for side, CO 1 (2, 4, 6, 7, 10, 9) sts for underarm, work to end—126 (146, 166, 186, 198, 214, 226) sts. *Note: Make note of last row worked in Cable Pattern so you will know where to start when working the Sleeves.* Work even for 2″, ending with a WS row.

Shape Waist (RS): Decrease 4 sts this row, then every 6 rows twice, as follows: [Work to 3 sts before marker, ssk, k1, sm, k1, k2tog] twice, work to end—114 (134, 154, 174, 186, 202, 214) sts remain. Work even until piece measures 13 (14, 14½, 15½, 16, 16½, 17)″ from the beginning, ending with a WS row.

Next Row (RS): Change to 2×2 Rib. Work even for 4½″. BO all sts loosely in pattern.

SLEEVES

Note: Use your preferred method of working in the rnd when working the Sleeves (see page 150).

Transfer Sleeve sts from waste yarn to needle(s). With RS facing, rejoin yarn at underarm; begin St st, work to end, working Cable Pattern as you come to it, beginning with rnd following last row worked on Body, pick up and knit 1 (2, 4, 6, 7, 10, 9) sts from sts CO for underarm, pm for beginning of rnd, pick up and knit 1 (2, 4, 6, 7, 10, 9) sts from sts CO for underarm, work to end of rnd—50 (62, 68, 80, 86, 94, 98) sts. Join for working in the rnd. Work even for 2 rnds.

Shape Sleeve: Decrease 2 sts this rnd, every 4 (2, 2, 2, 2, 2, 2) rnds 2 (4, 8, 14, 16, 22, 16) times, then every 6 (4, 4, 4, 4, 0, 4) rnds 4 (6, 5, 3, 2, 0, 4) times, as follows: K1, k2tog, k1, ssk–36 (40, 40, 44, 48, 48, 56) sts remain. Work even until Sleeve measures 6 (6, 6½, 7, 7¼, 7½, 8½)" from underarm.

Next Rnd: Change to 2x2 Rib in-the-Round. Work even for 3". BO all sts loosely in pattern.

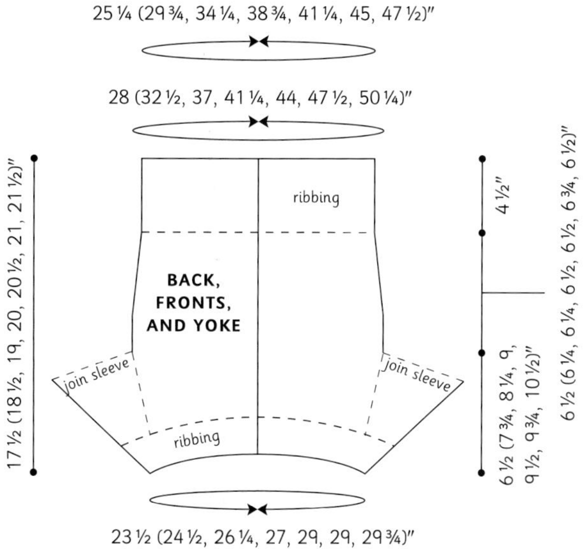

25¼ (29¾, 34¼, 38¾, 41¼, 45, 47½)"
28 (32½, 37, 41¼, 44, 47½, 50¼)"
ribbing
BACK, FRONTS, AND YOKE
join sleeve
join sleeve
ribbing
17½ (18½, 19, 20, 20½, 21, 21½)"
4½"
6½ (7¾, 8¼, 9, 9½, 9¾, 10½)"
6½ (6¼, 6¼, 6½, 6½, 6¾, 6½)"
23½ (24½, 26¼, 27, 29, 29, 29¾)"

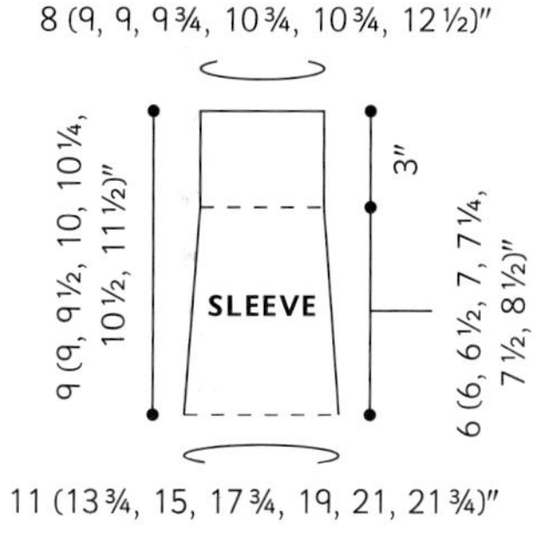

8 (9, 9, 9¾, 10¾, 10¾, 12½)"
9 (9, 9½, 10, 10¼, 10½, 11½)"
3"
SLEEVE
6 (6, 6½, 7, 7¼, 7½, 8½)"
11 (13¾, 15, 17¾, 19, 21, 21¾)"

FINISHING

Sew underarm seams. Weave in all ends.

Button Band: With RS facing, pick up and knit 82 (86, 90, 90, 90, 94, 94) sts along Left Front. Begin 2x2 Rib. Work even for 2". BO all sts loosely in pattern.

Buttonhole Band: Place markers for buttons on Right Front, the first ½" from the top, the last ½" from the bottom, and the remaining 5 (5, 5, 6, 6, 6, 6) evenly spaced between. Work as for Button Band until Band measures ¾", ending with a WS row.

Buttonhole Row (RS): Work to first buttonhole marker, *BO 2 sts, work to next marker; repeat from * to last marker, BO 2 sts, work to end. Work even until Band measures 2", CO 2 sts over BO sts on first row using Backward Loop CO (see Special Techniques, page 162). BO all sts loosely in pattern. Sew buttons opposite buttonholes.

Block piece if desired.

MAKE IT YOUR OWN

If you want cap sleeves instead of the ones shown, transfer the Sleeve stitches from waste yarn to needle(s), as directed at the start of the Sleeves section in the pattern, and work a couple rounds even, then work a round with paired decreases in the center underarm (k1, k2tog, work to 3 sts before marker, ssk, k1). Work a plain round, and then another decrease round. Try on as you go so you can tell how it will fit—at least 2 decrease rounds will be needed for a good fit. Then switch to smaller needles for your ribbing and bind off.

FINISHED MEASUREMENTS

20″ circumference, slightly
stretched

YARN

Jo Sharp Alpaca Kid Lustre
(30% superfine alpaca / 40%
kid mohair / 30% merino; 120
yards / 50 grams): 2 balls #852
vintage (MC)

Cherry Tree Hill Glitter Alpaca
(99% alpaca / 1% metallic;
232 yards / 50 grams): 1 hank
potluck water (A)

NEEDLES

One pair straight needles size
US 5 (3.75 mm)

One pair straight needles size
US 6 (4 mm)

Change needle size if necessary
to obtain correct gauge.

GAUGE

20 sts and 24 rows = 4″ (10 cm)
in Stockinette stitch (St st) using
larger needles

INSTANT GLAMOUR

Okay, I'll admit it: I've always been a little wary of stranded colorwork.
But for this book, I wanted to include a project that gives a beginning
knitter the perfect opportunity to try it out in a safe, low-risk environ-
ment. I figured out how many stitches were needed for the beret, then
I fiddled around with some graph paper and figured out a simple two-
color Fair Isle pattern that would add just enough interest to make the
beret sing. A lot of the colorwork I like features three colors or more,
so I sort of cheated by using a solid main color and a variegated, glittery
contrasting color. But, let's be honest, whatever way you knit it . . . talk
about instant glamour!

PATTERN FEATURES
Stranded colorwork, reading charts

STITCH PATTERN

1×1 Rib
(multiple of 2 sts; 1-row repeat)
All Rows: *K1, p1; repeat from * to end.

NOTES

This beret is worked flat, but if you want to convert it to an in-the-round pattern, it's easy. Cast on 84 stitches, join for working in the round, place marker. Work as given in the pattern until you've completed Chart A. Work even for 4 rounds, but don't increase 1 stitch on each side on the last round (these are edge stitches and you don't need them when you work in the round)–126 stitches. After you've worked Chart B twice, work even as indicated, but don't decrease 1 stitch on each side on the last round. Complete as directed, working rounds instead of rows. When you're done, thread your yarn tail through the remaining 12 stitches, pull tight and fasten off.

BERET

Using smaller needles and A, CO 84 sts. Change to MC and 1×1 Rib. Work even until piece measures 1½", ending with a WS row.

Increase Row (RS): Change to larger needles. K1, m1, *k2, m1; repeat from * to last st, k1—126 sts. Work even in St st for 3 rows.

Begin Charts

Next Row (RS): Begin Chart A, changing colors as indicated. Work 1 vertical repeat of Chart A. Change

to MC and St st. Work even for 4 rows, increase 1 st each side on last row—128 sts. *Note: Do not cut A; run it loosely up the outside edge.*

Next Row (RS): *K1 (edge st, keep in St st), work Chart B, changing colors as indicated, to last st, k1 (edge st, keep in St st). Work 1 vertical repeat of Chart. Change to MC and St st. Work even for 1 row. Repeat from * once. Work even for 4 rows, decrease 1 st each side on last row—126 sts remain.

Next Row (RS): Change to Chart A. Work 1 vertical repeat of Chart, decrease 1 st at end of last row—125 sts remain. *Note: This means that the last repeat of the Chart will be incomplete.*

Shape Hat

Note: In some instances you will be working decreases on the same row as the Chart. If you are not comfortable doing both, simply discontinue working the Chart once you've begun the decreases. Because of the decreases, on some rows, you will have an odd number of sts and will not be able to complete the last repeat of the Chart.

Decrease Row 1 (RS): *K3, k2tog; repeat from * to end—100 sts remain. Work even for 3 rows.

Decrease Row 2 (RS): Work Chart A and AT THE SAME TIME, *k2, k2tog; repeat from * to end—75 sts remain. Work even for 3 rows, working Row 2 of Chart A on first row.

Decrease Row 3 (RS): *K1, k2tog; repeat from * to end—50 sts remain. Work even for 3 rows.

Decrease Row 4 (RS): Work Chart A and AT THE SAME TIME, *k2tog; repeat from * to end—25 sts remain. Work even for 3 rows, working Row 2 of Chart A on first row.

Decrease Row 5 (RS): *K2tog; repeat from * to last three sts, k3tog—12 sts remain. Cut yarn, leaving a 12" tail; thread through remaining sts, pull tight and fasten off.

FINISHING

Using yarn tail, sew back seam from top to bottom. Block as desired.

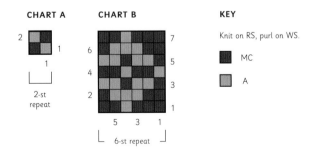

MAKE IT YOUR OWN

The beret, as written, has a ton of attitude, so for those who want a little less zest, it's easy to reduce the amount of slouch. All you have to do is follow the pattern as written, except instead of working Chart B twice, work it only one time. Continue to the next step in the pattern. This will result in a shorter, more modest cap.

This variation was worked with 2 hanks of Classic Elite Yarns Miracle (50% alpaca / 50% tencel; 108 yards / 50 grams) in #3304 Palm Beach blue. The contrast color was worked with the same color of yarn featured in the main pattern.

KARMA

I designed this tank on the fly from the bottom up using a stitch pattern book and a little imagination. First, I chose the German Herringbone Rib stitch pattern from *A Second Treasury of Knitting Patterns* by Barbara G. Walker. Then I chose my yarn and knit a swatch in order to figure out my stitch gauge and the width of one repeat/vertical herringbone panel, which was the information I needed in order to ascertain how many panels I needed to start with at the bottom edge (the widest point) and how many I needed to decrease to at the bust (the narrowest point). To give myself a place to decrease that wouldn't disrupt the herringbone pattern, I adjusted my numbers to allow for 5 extra purl stitches between each panel. Once I finished knitting the tank top, I knew I wanted to design the skirt variation, which is shown on page 136. I achieved this by adding more panels to accommodate a larger circumference at the bottom edge and then decreasing up to the waist. Instructions for both the tank top and the skirt are given in the pattern.

SIZES

X-Small (Small, Medium, Large, 1X-Large, 2X-Large, 3X-Large)

FINISHED MEASUREMENTS

Tank: 32 (34, 36, 40, 42, 46, 50)" chest

Skirt: 35¾ (39, 41¼, 45½, 48¾, 52, 55¼)" hip

YARN

Louet Sales Euroflax Athens (100% linen; 200 yards / 100 grams): Tank: 3 (4, 4, 4, 5, 5, 6) hanks #18.21026 moss lake; Skirt: 4 (4, 4, 5, 5, 5, 6) hanks #18.21046 purple mysterie

NEEDLES

One 32" (82 cm) long or longer circular (circ) needle size US 6 (4 mm)

One pair double-pointed needles (dpn) size US 6 (4 mm), for Tank

Change needle size if necessary to obtain correct gauge.

NOTIONS

Stitch markers in 2 colors

GAUGE

20 sts and 24 rows = 4" (10 cm) in Stockinette stitch (St st)

NOTES

This pattern is for both the Tank and the Skirt variation on page 136. The first set of figures is for the Tank; the second set of figures, shown between <>, is for the Skirt. Where only one set of figures is given, it applies to both the Tank and the Skirt.

BODY

With circ needle, CO 18 sts, [place marker (pm), CO 18 sts] 9 (10, 11, 12, 13, 14, 15) <11 (12, 13, 14, 15, 16, 17)> times—180 (198, 216, 234, 252, 270, 288) <198 (216, 234, 252, 270, 288, 306)> sts. Join for working in the rnd, being careful not to twist sts, pm (different color) for beginning of rnd.

> PATTERN FEATURES
> Bottom-up construction, body and skirt worked in the round, long-repeat stitch pattern, I-Cord

STITCH PATTERN

German Herringbone Rib
(panel of 13 sts; 6-rnd repeat)
Rnd 1: M1, k3, p2, p3tog, p2, k3, m1.
Rnd 2: K4, p5, k4.
Rnd 3: M1, k4, p1, p3tog, p1, k4, m1.
Rnd 4: K5, p3, k5.
Rnd 5: M1, k5, p3tog, k5, m1.
Rnd 6: K6, p1, k6.
Repeat Rnds 1-6 for German Herringbone Rib.

Begin Pattern: Work 13 sts in German Herringbone Rib, p5, *slip marker (sm), work 13 sts in German Herringbone Rib, p5; repeat from * around. Work even for 23 <41> rnds [you should have completed 4 <7> vertical repeats of German Herringbone Rib].

Decrease Rnd 1: Work 13 sts in German Herringbone Rib, p2tog, p3, *sm, work 13 sts in German Herringbone Rib, p2tog, p3; repeat from * around—170 (187, 204, 221, 238, 255, 272) <187 (204, 221, 238, 255, 272, 289)> sts remain [17 sts between markers]. Work even for 11 <17> rnds [you should have completed 6 <10> vertical repeats of German Herringbone Rib].

Decrease Rnd 2: Work 13 sts in German Herringbone Rib, p2tog, p2, *sm, work 13 sts in German Herringbone Rib, p2tog, p2; repeat from * around—160 (176, 192, 208, 224, 240, 256) <176 (192, 208, 224, 240, 256, 272)> sts remain [16 sts between markers]. Work even for 5 <17> rnds [you should have completed 7 <13> vertical repeat(s) of German Herringbone Rib].

Decrease Rnd 3: Work 13 sts in German Herringbone Rib, p2tog, p1, *sm, work 13 sts in German Herringbone Rib, p2tog, p1; repeat from * around—150 (165, 180, 195, 210, 225, 240) <165 (180, 195, 210, 225, 240, 255)> sts remain [15 sts between markers]. Work even for 17 (23, 23, 23, 29, 29, 29) <11> rnds [you should have completed 10 (11, 11, 11, 12, 12, 12) <15> vertical repeats of German Herringbone Rib].

Next Rnd: Change to Rev St st (purl every rnd). Work even for 3 rnds, removing all markers on first rnd except beginning of rnd marker.

Tank Only:

BODICE

Next Rnd: Change to St st (knit every rnd), inc 10 (5, 0, 5, 0, 5, 10) sts evenly spaced on first rnd—160 (170, 180, 200, 210, 230, 250) sts. Knit 1 rnd, pm after 80 (85, 90, 100, 105, 115, 125) sts for side. Work even until Bodice measures 2 ½ (3, 3, 3, 3 ½, 3 ½, 4)″, or to just below point of bust, measured from beginning of St st.

Shape Bust

Note: Bust will be shaped using Short Rows (see Special Techniques, page 162). Hide all wraps as you come to them. You may omit the short-row shaping, if preferred.

Row 1 (RS): Knit to 6 sts before next marker, slip 1, wrp-t.

Row 2: Purl to 6 sts before next marker, slip 1, wrp-t.

Repeat Rows 1 and 2 one (one, one, one, two, two, two) time(s). *Note: If you have a bra cup size of C or larger, consider working additional short rows, trying piece on until you like the fit.* Work even until Bodice measures 6 (6 ½, 7, 7 ½, 8, 8 ½, 9)" measured at underarm, or to desired length from beginning of St st, decrease 10 sts evenly spaced on last rnd—150 (160, 170, 190, 200, 220, 240) sts remain. *Note: If you wish the top of the Bodice to fit more tightly, decrease more than 10 sts.* Purl 2 rnds. BO all sts loosely purlwise.

FINISHING

Straps: Try on Tank and mark desired placement of two front Straps. *Note: You may also lay a favorite camisole on top of the Tank and copy placement of its straps to the Tank.* With RS facing, using dpn, pick up and knit 3 sts centered over first Strap marker. Begin 3-st I-Cord (see Special Techniques, page 162). Work even until I-Cord measures 11", or to desired length. Fasten off, leaving a 6" long tail. Repeat for opposite Strap. Do not sew end to Back. Machine wash and dry Tank, and carefully steam-iron. *Note: If using substituted yarn, block according to manufacturer's directions.* Try on Tank and mark where Straps should be attached to Back. If needed, shorten Straps by unraveling I-Cord. Sew Straps to Back at markers.

Skirt Only:

Next Rnd: Change to St st (knit every rnd). Work even until piece measures 4 ½" from beginning of St st, dec 5 (4, 3, 2, 1, 0, 7) sts evenly spaced across last rnd—160 (176, 192, 208, 224, 240, 248) sts remain.

Eyelet Rnd: *K2, yo, k2tog; repeat from * around. Knit 1 rnd. BO all sts loosely.

FINISHING

Cord Tie: Cut 2 strands of yarn 4 times waist measurement (or at least 3 times desired finished length). With both strands held together, work Twisted Cord (see Special Techniques, page 162). Beginning and ending at center front, thread Cord through Eyelet Row. Block as desired.

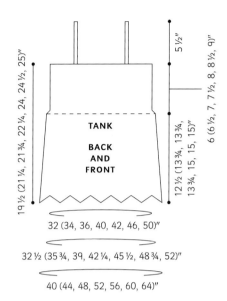

TANK

BACK AND FRONT

5 ½"

6 (6 ½, 7, 7 ½, 8, 8 ½, 9)"

12 ½ (13 ¾, 13 ¾, 13 ¾, 15, 15, 15)"

19 ½ (21 ¼, 21 ¾, 22 ¼, 24, 24 ½, 25)"

32 (34, 36, 40, 42, 46, 50)"

32 ½ (35 ¾, 39, 42 ¼, 45 ½, 48 ¾, 52)"

40 (44, 48, 52, 56, 60, 64)"

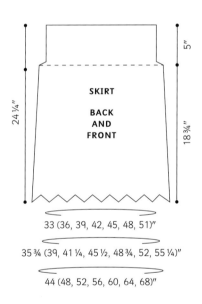

SKIRT

BACK AND FRONT

5"

18 ¾"

24 ¼"

33 (36, 39, 42, 45, 48, 51)"

35 ¾ (39, 41 ¼, 45 ½, 48 ¾, 52, 55 ¼)"

44 (48, 52, 56, 60, 64, 68)"

CHAPTER 6

Unleash Your Inner Designer: Elements to Alter and Starting from Scratch

Sometimes you'll want to make big changes to an existing pattern and in the process "unleash your inner designer," and sometimes you'll want to make small changes, to simply customize an existing pattern so it works for you perfectly. And occasionally—especially once you gain some confidence with alterations—you may even want to design your own sweaters from scratch. In this chapter I provide an overview of how top-down sweaters are constructed, review the elements that you can change each step of the way, and provide basic formulas for three classic sweater styles to knit from scratch.

TOP-DOWN OVERVIEWS

Here's a quick explanation of how I construct the two types of top-down sweater styles featured in this book.

TOP-DOWN RAGLAN

TOP-DOWN SET-IN SLEEVE

TOP-DOWN RAGLAN OVERVIEW

This type of sweater begins with stitches cast on for the neck opening. You then join to work in the round for a pullover, or work back and forth for a cardigan, creating a seamless rounded rectangular yoke with a center "hole" for the neck opening. Note that if the pattern has a shaped neckline, you will not join to work in the round until neck shaping is complete (see Neckbands and Collars on page 142). Increases are made into each "corner" of the yoke every other row (for a cardigan) or every other round (for a pullover). When the rounded rectangle is big enough to cover your shoulders down to your underarm, you divide it into sleeves, a back, and a front. The shorter sides become your sleeves and the longer sides become your back and front(s). The sleeve stitches are placed on hold, then the back is connected to the front(s) and worked either back and forth (for a cardigan) or in the round (for a pullover) down to the hem. After binding off the hem, the sleeve stitches are placed back on the needles and worked in the round down to the cuff. The neckband or cardigan edging is added last. For a formula for how to do a simple top-down raglan without a pattern, see page 154.

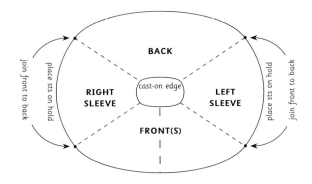

TOP-DOWN SET-IN SLEEVE OVERVIEW

The top-down set-in sleeve sweater is really just a sleeveless and seamless shell or vest, or the beginning of what will become a top with "afterthought" sleeves. To work a garment this way, you begin at the shoulder tops using a provisional cast-on (see Special Techniques, page 162; note that the provisional cast-on isn't absolutely necessary but helps to avoid bulky shoulder seams) and work your way down the back to just under the arms, adding armhole shaping along the way. These stitches are then placed on hold.

Next the shoulder stitches are placed back on the needles, leaving the center back neck stitches on hold. For a cardigan, the fronts are worked separately down to the armholes. After armhole shaping is added, fronts are joined to the back under the arms and the piece is worked back and forth to the hem. For a pullover, the front sections are worked separately down to where the chosen neckline will fall, the center front stitches are cast on, and the front is joined into one piece. Then armhole shaping is added and the front is joined to the back under the arms and worked in the round down to the hem.

Sleeves are added next by picking up stitches in the armhole, then worked in the round with some short-row shaping (see Special Techniques, page 162) for the sleeve cap and continued down to the cuff. Neckbands or cardigan edgings are added last. For a formula for how to make a top-down sweater with set-in sleeves without a pattern, see page 156.

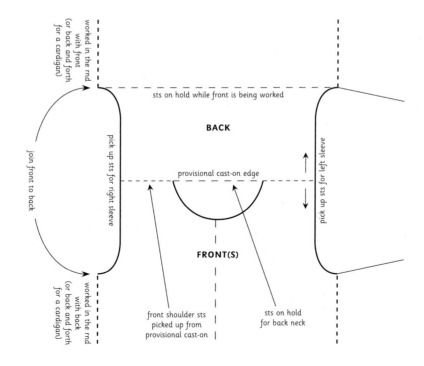

ELEMENTS TO ALTER

The patterns in this book were designed so that common elements like collar or neckline treatment, sleeve style, waist shaping, or length can be changed or completely revamped, if you so desire. Once you have a basic understanding of top-down construction (see page 140), refer to this section to discover what elements are changeable and when the time is right to change them.

Alteration 1: Neckbands and Collars

Almost all of the top-down constructions featured in this book work similarly in that the neckline comes first, rather than last, as in bottom-up knitting. Many of the collars are worked at the very end by picking up stitches around the neckline after the garment body is completed, offering a multitude of opportunities for customization after the rest of the sweater is done. Following are instructions for the most popular types of alterations.

V-NECK TO CREWNECK IN TOP-DOWN KNITTING

Let's say you have a pattern for a basic V-neck top-down sweater (like Pink on page 22). Changing it into a crewneck is simple and straightforward.

1 Work the pattern as it is written until the sides of the front reach approximately 4 rows from where you want the neck of the sweater to end.

2 Count the stitches on the back and the stitches on the 2 fronts. Subtract the stitches on the 2 fronts from the stitches on the back; this is the number of stitches you will have to cast on or increase over the next few rows.

3 On the next 2 right-side rows, cast on 2 or 3 stitches at each neck edge (fewer stitches for a heavier gauge yarn; more stitches for a finer gauge yarn). If you want a deeper crewneck, work another 2 right-side rows and add another 2 or 3 stitches as you did on the previous rows.

4 If you're making a pullover, at the end of the next right-side row, cast on the remaining stitches required to make the two fronts equal to the back. If you're making a cardigan, on the next row, cast on to each of the fronts half of the total stitches required to make the 2 fronts equal to the back. For instance, if the back has 70 stitches and the fronts each have 25 stitches, you need an additional 20 stitches to make the fronts equal the back; so you will cast on 10 stitches on each front. If you are not planning on adding front bands, you may wish to cast on additional stitches to each front so that they overlap in the center.

5 Join the work for a pullover or continue working back and forth for a cardigan, and follow the rest of the pattern as written, ignoring the neckline instructions. When the body and sleeves are complete, add the neckband or collar edging of your choice (see page 144).

CREWNECK TO V-NECK IN TOP-DOWN KNITTING

Changing a crewneck into a V-neck is simple, but requires a little forethought. Basically, you need to know in advance if you want a shallow or a deep V-neck.

1 Work the pattern as it is written until the fronts reach the inside edge of your shoulders, just at the base of your neck. Note that this may mean that you begin shaping very soon after casting on or picking up from your provisional cast-on.

2 If you're like me and like to work your increases in a very simple way, begin increasing a stitch at each neckline edge on every fourth row for a deep V-neck. For a shallower V-neck, increase on every third row, which means you will be working some of the increases on right-side rows and some of them on wrong-side rows. For a very shallow V-neck, increase on every right-side row.

Should you want to be more precise, how often you work increases will depend on the number of stitches you have to increase. For example, if you are working a shallow neck with a finer weight yarn, you may need to work increases more often in order to complete the shaping before you get to the desired neck depth. You can determine how often to increase with a mathematical formula: First divide the number of rows you have available to you for shaping by 2 (this will allow you to work increases on right-side rows only). Then take the resulting number and divide it by the number of stitches you have to increase. The final number will tell you how many rows to work in between increases. If you end up with a number under 1, then you will have to increase more than 1 stitch per row until you have the required number of stitches for the neck. If you end up with a number between 1 and 2, then you will have to work a portion of the increases on every other row and the rest on every row. If your final number is a whole number (for example 2, 4, or 6), you will work an increase every 2, 4, or 6 rows. If your final number is a fraction higher than 2 (like 3.6), and you want to be wildly precise, you must round it both up and down to the nearest whole number divisible by 2 (in this case, 4 and 2). You will then have to work a portion of the increases on every fourth row, and the remaining increases on every other row. I'm not a big fan of plotting out this sort of thing on graph paper, but if you're the type, go for it.

3 Continue until there are as many total stitches on the 2 front sections as there are on the back (or to your desired number if you prefer overlapping fronts for a cardigan). Note that if you want a very deep V-neck that ends below the armholes, you will have to continue the neck shaping after working the armhole shaping.

4 Join the work for a pullover or continue working back and forth for a cardigan, and follow the rest of the pattern as written, ignoring the neckline instructions. When the body and sleeves are complete, add the neckband or collar edging of your choice (see page 144).

CREWNECK OR V-NECK TO SQUARE NECKLINE IN TOP-DOWN KNITTING

Not only are square necklines flattering to most body types, they are probably the easiest of all necklines to make.

1 Work the pattern as it is written, omitting any neck increases, until the front sides are the desired neck depth minus the depth of whatever ribbing you will add.

2 Subtract the stitches on the 2 sides of the front from the stitches on the back to get the number of stitches you will need to add on to make the front equal to the back.

3 If you're making a pullover, on the end of the next right-side row, cast on enough stitches to make the two front sides equal to the back. If you're making a cardigan, on the next row, cast on to each of the fronts half of the total stitches required to make the two fronts equal to the back, then follow the pattern as written, ignoring the neckline instructions for the V-neck. For instance, if the back has 70 stitches and the fronts each have 20 stitches, you need an additional 30 stitches to make the fronts equal the back, so you will cast on 15 stitches on each front. If you are not planning on adding front bands, you may wish to cast on additional stitches to each front so that they overlap in the center.

4 Join the work for a pullover or continue working back and forth for a cardigan, and follow the rest of the pattern as written, ignoring the neckline instructions. When the body and sleeves are complete, add a square neckband edging (see page 144).

Common Neckbands and Collars

Once you have finished your garment, you can add just about any neckband or collar you want, provided the shape of the opening accommodates it. There are a couple of common methods for working a neckband, including picking up stitches and working it in the round, or working it separately and sewing it on later (which requires a bit more fussing).

Whenever you pick up stitches, make sure that you pick up approximately 2 stitches for every 3 stitches or rows and in a multiple that fits the ribbing you've planned. This isn't a hard and fast rule, but this ratio usually works for me—if you find that your knitting doesn't lay flat or puckers, start over and adjust. Also, if there is any chance that the line or "seam" of picked up stitches will show on the wrong side after the edging is complete (for example, with a collar and neckline that lie open), pick up and knit the stitches with the wrong side of the garment facing you.

Note that whatever edging you add, the neck opening must be large enough to fit over your head. And, especially if you are working a close-fitting opening, be sure that you either bind off in ribbing or bind off loosely enough that the neck opening will be elastic.

V-NECK EDGINGS

Overlapping V-Neck: For a V-neckband that overlaps, pick up stitches evenly beginning at the center "V", and work in a rib pattern back and forth for the desired neck depth. Bind off in pattern and tack the right side over the left for a woman's garment or vice versa for a man's.

Flat V-Neck with a Center Stitch: For a V-neckband that lies flat, pick up stitches evenly around and mark the center stitch. Working in the round, on every round, work to 2 stitches before the marked stitch, ssk, knit the center stitch, k2tog, work to the end of the round. Repeat this round until your neckband is the desired depth. Bind off in pattern.

V-Neck Cardigan: You can work your neckband and front bands at the same time. Just work the band by picking up stitches around the entire piece, beginning at the lower right front edge and ending at the lower left front edge. If your circular needle isn't long enough to reach around the garment and you don't want to use a series of circulars to accommodate all the stitches, you can split the piece at the center back neck and sew the edges of the band together after you have bound off.

SQUARE NECKBAND EDGING

Pick up stitches around the neckline with a short circular needle, starting at one shoulder. You'll want to pick up about 2 stitches for every 3 rows at the side edges, and make sure that you pick up an odd number of stitches on each front side edge, the center front, and the back, and that you have an odd number of stitches between your corner stitches on the front edge. Mark your corner stitches; these should be knit stitches when you work the ribbing.

On every round, work in 1×1 ribbing to 1 stitch before the marked stitch *slip the next stitch and marked stitch together as if to k2tog (removing the marker), knit 1 stitch, pass the 2 slipped stitches over the knit stitch, reposition the marker before the stitch just made, work to 1 stitch before the next marked stitch; repeat from the * once, then work to the end of the round. Repeat this round to the desired neck depth. Bind off in pattern.

CREWNECK EDGINGS

Single and Double Crewneck: A single crewneck is just a simple ribbing that is added after the body of the sweater is completed and in one piece. Work a single crewneck on circular or double-pointed needles that are 1 or 2 sizes smaller than those used for the rest of the garment, and pick up stitches evenly (2 stitches for every 3 stitches or rows and in a multiple that fits the ribbing) around the neckline. When choosing a rib pattern, use the ribbing on the rest of the garment for inspiration. Work the collar to the desired depth and bind off loosely. To make a double crewneck, just work to double the desired depth, then sew the bound-off edge to the inside at the pick-up row/round.

Turtleneck: A turtleneck is essentially an extended crewneck. It is usually ribbed and can be worked exactly the same as the crewneck except you will want to change to larger needles as you progress toward the top to prevent the folded edge from riding up. Bind off loosely. Most turtlenecks are approximately 7 or 8" long.

Open Collar/Mandarin Collar: For an open collar that lies down like a polo collar, begin picking up stitches at the center front, and work the collar back and forth in ribbing to the desired depth. Bind off loosely. You can also make an open collar that overlaps in the front. To do this, pick up neckband stitches beginning an inch to the right of the center of the front, and at the end of the first row, cast on for an additional 1¾". Work in ribbing for approximately 4", or longer depending on the look you want to achieve, and bind off the stitches. Overlap the added stitches and tack them down behind the picked-up stitches. For a Mandarin version of the open collar, pick up stitches as for a polo collar, but begin picking up stitches about ½" outside the center front (for a pullover, leave an opening of about 1" in the center front) and work the collar back and forth until it is 1 or 2" long. A Mandarin collar can be tricky because unless it is worked in a tight gauge and close to the neck, it may be too floppy. Be sure to work your collar on a smaller needle and use firmer yarn too, if possible.

Side Split Collar: Pick up stitches, beginning and ending at one shoulder, and work a flat ribbing like 2×2 or 3×1. Increase a few stitches at one shoulder seam by casting on to overlap the split. Work back and forth without joining. For a neat edge, keep the first and last stitches in Stockinette stitch. (Since the first row after the pick-up is a wrong side row, you should begin and end with a purl stitch, not a knit stitch.) When the collar is your desired length, bind off in pattern and tack down the overlapping portion at the shoulder seam.

Crewneck Cardigan: After the front bands are complete, pick up and knit stitches around the neck, beginning at the right front band edge. Working in the same edging as the front bands, work back and forth until you reach the desired depth. If you want, you can add a buttonhole in the neckband to match those on the button band.

OVERLAPPING V-NECK

DOUBLE CREWNECK

TURTLENECK

CREWNECK CARDIGAN

Alteration 2: Armhole Depth

It's easy to alter the armhole depth on garments worked in the round from the top down. Just try on as you go and when the garment is almost long enough to reach the bottom of the armpit, work your armhole shaping. Join the body in the round once the armhole shaping is complete. Garments worked in the round from the bottom up offer a similar opportunity—in this case, just try on as you go and when it reaches your armpit, begin your armhole shaping, and separate the front and back into two sides. From there, work up to the shoulders.

ADJUSTING ARMHOLES IN TOP-DOWN SWEATERS

Set-In Sleeve Sweaters: If you want a longer or shorter armhole opening in a top-down set-in sleeve sweater, just look ahead to "Shape Armholes" in the pattern you're following and count the number of rows that make up the shaping portion of the opening. Using your row gauge as a guide, convert the number of shaping rows into inches. In most cases—at least in this book—you will be working the back portion of the sweater first, so hold the garment up to your body as you knit and when the garment reaches your desired armhole depth minus the distance the shaping rows will add to it, begin your armhole shaping as written in the pattern. Place a safety pin or removable marker where you begin your shaping so when it is time to work the front you can start the shaping at the same point in the knitting.

Note that if you have adjusted your armhole depth, you will also be picking up a different number of sleeve stitches around the opening. Read Afterthought Sleeves on page 150 for tips on working these types of sleeves using your new stitch count. Also make note of the number of inches you subtracted or added to the underarm and take this into account as you compare your sweater to the pattern schematics you have been following.

Raglan Sweaters: Top-down raglan armholes are a little different—if you suspect the armhole depth will be too short or too long, the best way to adjust it is to work the pattern, as written, until you can spread the yoke over your shoulder-points, and the raglan increase columns have been established and are reaching down toward the underarm. Drape the yoke over your shoulders, and lay a tape measure along one raglan increase column and extend its diagonal line to about an inch below where you want your armhole to fall to find out how many more inches you have to go. If you are following the standard rate of increasing at each element around the yoke—2 stitches increased for the front (or 1 stitch for each front if you're working a cardigan), 2 for each sleeve, and 2 for the back—you will be adding 8 stitches on each increase row or round, usually on every right-side row or every other round. Note that although this is the standard rate of increasing, the number is definitely adjustable, so you have some flexibility.

Multiply the number of inches you have to go to reach your desired underarm length by your row gauge to find out how many rows/rounds still need to be worked. Divide this number by 2 to determine the number of actual increase rows/rounds you will work (since you are increasing every other row/round). Multiply this number by 8, and you will have the number of stitches you are going to increase over the following rows/rounds, assuming you continue to increase as you have been (8 stitches every other row/round). If the total number of stitches that you end up with is too many or too few to accommodate your chest size, then space your increases to the front and the back sections farther apart (maybe every 4 rows/rounds instead of every other) or closer together (every row/round instead of every other) in order to accommodate. Note that as you work the following increase rows/rounds, you will continue to work increases to the sleeve sections every other row/round as you've been doing.

For example, let's say you want to lengthen your raglan increase columns, but you realize that if you lengthen them and work the increases every row/round as established, you will end up with too many stitches on the body sections, thus a sweater that is too big. So you need to work fewer increases on the front and back sections than on the sleeve sections.

To begin to calculate the spacing of the front and back increases, first determine how many stitches you need on the front and back at each underarm to give you the desired chest measurement. Divide this number by 2 to get the number of stitches each for the front and back. Subtract the number of stitches now on the front or back from the desired number for that section, and divide the final number by 2 to give you the number of 2-stitch increases (1 stitch at each raglan increase column) you need to make to get to the desired number of stitches for that section. Divide the number of rows/rounds still to be worked by the number of 2-stitch increases to be worked. This will tell you how far apart the remaining increase rounds must be. You may be increasing every fourth row/round, or every fifth, from here on, instead of working the increases every other row/round as you will continue to do for the sleeves. As you do this, always keep track of how many stitches you added or subtracted to each element so that if the sweater body requires a particular multiple of stitches for a stitch pattern, you will know to make a few decreases or increases to bring your stitch count to that multiple.

ADJUSTING ARMHOLES IN BOTTOM-UP SWEATERS

When working a sweater from the bottom up, provided the neckline shaping is straightforward, adjusting the depth of the armhole is relatively easy. Simply decide on the depth you want your armhole to be and subtract the called-for number of inches from the desired depth to find out the number of inches to add to or subtract from the measurement given in the pattern. After you have completed your armhole shaping, continue working the armhole to the desired new depth and add the neckline shaping as called for in the pattern. Make note of your new measurements so when you work the other side of the garment, you'll remember what you did.

RAGLAN SWEATER
WITH STANDARD-FITTING ARMHOLES

RAGLAN SWEATER
WITH CLOSE-FITTING ARMHOLES

Alteration 3: Length and Shaping

Making changes to the general length and shape of the garments in this book is simple. Since the front(s) and the back are worked together, you simply stop knitting or keep going if you want to shorten or lengthen your garment. If you would like to shorten a garment after the fact, just unravel bound-off stitches to the correct length, put the stitches back on your needles, add your new edging, and bind off again. The same idea applies to long sleeves when they are worked from the top down.

Bear in mind that when you are working in the round and you want to change the garment's length, you will also need to make sure that when the perfect length is reached, the circumference is also perfect. For smooth, subtle shaping, you will want to space the decreases or increases evenly between the wider and narrower sections.

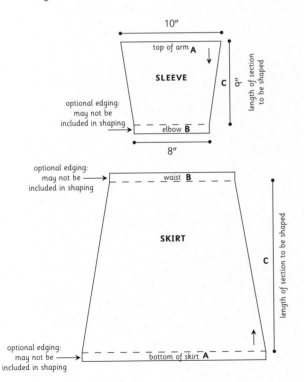

ADJUSTING SHAPING

This simple calculation can be used for shaping sweaters, sleeves, skirts, or any other knitted item that requires shaping.

1 Make a test swatch in the stitch pattern and yarn you will be using, and determine the number of stitches and rows to the inch. For this exercise, let's say that our test swatch measures 5 stitches and 6 rows to the inch.

2 Measure the circumference, or width, of the point at which you want to begin shaping (for instance, the bottom of the skirt or the top of the sleeve), and the point at which you want to complete shaping (for example, the waist of the skirt or the wrist of the sleeve). If you are working from a pattern in this book, more likely than not, you will know the number of stitches at your starting point (the number of sleeve stitches that are currently on the needles when working a top-down raglan, or after working the cap shaping in a top-down set-in sleeve sweater). Divide this number of stitches by the stitch gauge of your test swatch to determine the circumference at this point. For example, let's say the number of stitches at the top of the arm is 50 (that means that it measures 10"), and you want your final circumference to be 8".

3 Subtract the smaller of these 2 measurements (B) from the larger (A), and multiply the result by your stitch gauge. That is 10" at the top of the arm and 8" at the elbow: 10" – 8" = 2".

2" × 5 stitches per inch = 10 stitches.

You will want to decrease 10 stitches between the widest and narrowest sections. Now, decide how many stitches you will be decreasing in each shaping row/round. In the case of the sleeve, 2 stitches are usually decreased in each decrease row/round, (1 stitch at the beginning, and 1 stitch at the end). This means that you will work 5 decreases (10 stitches ÷ 2 stitches decreased each row/round = 5 decreases).

4 Measure the vertical distance between the two sections (C) and multiply this result by your row gauge. For this example, the distance is 9″ from underarm to elbow, so 9″ × 6 rows/rounds per inch = 54 rows/rounds. This is how many rows/rounds it will take you to get from one level to another. *Note: If you are working any edging without shaping, be sure to subtract its length from the shaping distance before making this calculation.*

Divide the number of decreases you want to work into the number of rows/rounds you have to complete your decreases or increases. This is how you find out how many rows/rounds apart the shaping rows/rounds must be placed. Example: 54 rows/rounds ÷ 5 decreases = 10.8 rows/rounds. Round the resulting number up or down to the nearest whole number (11 in this case). Multiply that whole number by the number of decreases you need to work (11 × 5 = 55), and you get the number of rows/rounds you will have worked to complete the decreases. If your number is higher than the number of rows/rounds you have available for decreases, you may have to work 1 or more decreases at a lower number of rows/rounds; if the number is lower, you may have to work 1 or more decreases at a higher number of rows/rounds. For this example, 55 is 1 row/round more than we've allocated. We could either just work the 1 extra row/round, or we could work 1 decrease on the 10th row/round rather than the 11th. *Note: If you are working back and forth and prefer to keep all your decreases on right-side rows, simply round up or down to an even number.*

You can also use this formula when lengthening or shortening a skirt worked bottom-up, or to alter the circumference of its waistline. For example, if you want the waist (B) on your garment to be smaller than what the pattern calls for, subtract the number of stitches you want to end up with (since it is worked from the bottom up) from the number of stitches you start with (A). This is the number of stitches you need to decrease to end up with the proper number of stitches at the waist. Follow these 4 steps to determine the number of shaping units (or decrease rows/rounds) you will need in order to arrive at the correct waist circumference. Make note, however, that if there is a stitch pattern at the waist, your final number may need to be adjusted by a couple of stitches to accommodate it.

This formula also works in the reverse. If you are working from a narrower width to a wider one, the calculations are all the same; simply work increases instead of decreases.

SLEEVELESS SWEATER

AFTERTHOUGHT SLEEVES

Alteration 4: Afterthought Sleeves

All the sleeves in this book are worked either in one piece along with the garment or added on as afterthought sleeves. In many cases, they are picked up from the armholes and worked in the round, top down, or worked in the round from the cuff to the underarm. With any of these, you will have the opportunity to try on as you go and change the shape and length. Note that if you add a sleeve where there wasn't one, or increase the sleeve length or width, you may need more yarn (see Determining How Much Yarn to Buy, page 160).

This technique allows for a great deal of freedom when selecting patterns. If you know how to work an afterthought sleeve, then all you have to do, once the body of your garment is in one piece, is pick up stitches around the armhole, work your sleeve cap, then finish the sleeve the way you want to.

FORMULA FOR AFTERTHOUGHT SLEEVES

To work a seamless, set-in sleeve the way I like to do it—and the way many of the sleeves are constructed in this book—you'll need a circular needle or 2 for working in the round. If the armhole is large enough, I use a 16" long circular needle and work in the round. If the armhole is smaller, I use 2 circulars at once. Alternatively, you could work in the round using double-pointed needles. For an afterthought sleeve, you will need 6 markers in 3 colors.

1 Pick up and knit stitches evenly around the armhole, approximately 2 stitches for every 3 rows, marking the exact top of the shoulder with a marker as you go. Also place a marker in the same color at the bottom center of the armhole for the beginning of the round (do not use this color marker for any other purpose). You should have the same number of stitches on either side between the top of shoulder marker and the beginning of round marker (see illustration on facing page).

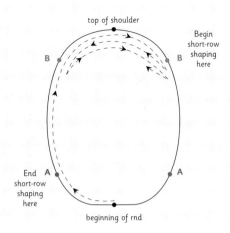

top of shoulder

Begin
short-row
shaping
here

B   B

End
short-row
shaping
here

A   A

beginning of rnd

2 Divide the number of stitches you picked up by 3 (rounding up or down to a number divisible by 2). This is the number of stitches you will have at the top of your sleeve cap, with half of these stitches on each side of the top of shoulder marker.

3 Note where on the back and front you began increasing stitches for your underarm shaping. (Refer to the pattern or look at the shaping of your armhole to identify those stitches. They will be single-stitch increases (m1's and cast-on stitches placed at the bottom of the underarm.)

4 Knit your way around the armhole (or begin the stitch pattern if there is one), and place a marker of a second color (call this marker A; see illustration) at the point where you *started* (if you worked the armhole from the top down) or *finished* (if you worked from the bottom up), adding underarm stitches either by increasing or casting on. Then, knowing how many stitches comprise a third of the total sleeve stitches, as you work, place 1 marker of a third color (call these markers B) before and after these stitches, remembering that half of the stitches should be on either side of the top of shoulder marker. Continue working around the armhole and place a marker of the second color (A) where you *started* (or *finished*) your underarm increases. *Note: You may, if you prefer, place removable markers in the appropriate places before you begin the second round. Or, after you have done this a few times, you may decide to omit the first knitted round and just place your markers as you initially pick up your stitches. This will produce an even smoother result. If, however, you are working a stitch pattern on the sleeves, it may help to work 1 round in the pattern before beginning the cap shaping.*

5 Take a look at your markers: You will see that you have a beginning of the round marker, 2 markers of the same color (A) on either side of the underarm stitches and 2 markers of the same color (B) marking the top third stitches, with a top of shoulder marker centered between them. (See illustration at left).

6 Now it is time to begin your short rows (see Special Techniques, page 162), which will shape the top of the sleeve. Having marked your armhole, work around the armhole, slipping the first 3 markers, all the way past the top of the sleeve to the farthest marker separating the top third of the sleeve from the rest of the stitches (B). Slip this marker and wrap the next stitch. Turn the work, and work across the wrong-side row across the center third of the sleeve (which has the top of shoulder marker in the middle of it) to the marker on the opposite side of the center third stitches (B), slip the marker and wrap the next stitch. Turn the work again, and work across the right-side row across the center third to 1 stitch beyond the place where you stopped before. Wrap the next stitch and turn. Again, work across the wrong-side row across the center third to 1 stitch beyond the previous stopping place, wrap the next stitch, and turn the work. Continue in this manner, working short rows back and forth across the sleeve cap and taking 1 more stitch from each side before you make a turn. Hide each wrapped stitch as you come to it (see Special Techniques, page 162).

7 When you have worked your way to the markers separating the underarm stitches from the others on both sides (A), you have completed the sleeve cap. Work a final right-side row across the remaining underarm stitches, hiding the leftover wrap as you come to it. Note that depending on how many stitches you cast on, and how you divided them up, you may find you have an extra stitch between your last wrapped stitch and the A marker. You may either work one more set of short rows, going just past the markers, or you may consider your short row shaping complete, and continue on.

8 Work your sleeve in the round, as desired, adding shaping as you go. Refer to Length and Shaping on page 148 for tips.

Alteration 5:
Pullover to Cardigan and Vice Versa

The only difference between a cardigan and a pullover is that a pullover is joined in the round while a cardigan is worked in rows that begin and end in the center front. A cardigan can be fastened with zippers, snaps, and buttons—even hooks and eyes.

TOP-DOWN PULLOVER TO CARDIGAN

Note that in most top-down pullover patterns, the number of back stitches and the number of front stitches are the same, once all the shaping is complete. With a cardigan, you have the option of working the fronts with or without front bands, which are typically added after the body and sleeves are complete. The finished fronts may meet at the center, or they may overlap. When the cardigan is overlapped in the front (if you choose not to work front bands) then each front must have stitches added that will allow them to overlap. If you are planning to work front bands, which are added on last, they can act as the overlapping material, so the number of front stitches won't need to be altered. *Note: If you are changing a pullover to a cardigan and plan on adding bands to your project, you will need more yarn than is called for in the existing pattern. See page 160 to estimate how much.* Armed with this knowledge, and assuming you want to retain the same neckline style as the one in your pattern, all you need to do is work the pullover pattern to the end of the neckline shaping. If you prefer to change the neckline used in the pattern, refer to Neckbands and Collars on page 142 for information on how to change neckline shaping. Then, instead of joining the two fronts as you would in a pullover, continue working the pattern as written, but in rows instead of rounds, working shaping rows as directed. *Note: This is where you would add more stitches if you wanted the fronts to overlap without having to work front bands.* When you are finished with the sleeves, work the neckline edging and front edges of your choice (see page 144). Add buttonholes to the right front of the bands for a woman's cardigan, or to the left front for a man's cardigan.

PULLOVER

CARDIGAN

TOP-DOWN CARDIGAN TO PULLOVER

Transforming a top-down cardigan into a pullover is just as straightforward as changing a pullover into a cardigan. The first thing you need to consider is whether or not the stitches on the 2 fronts, without the bands, will equal the number of stitches on the back. If they won't, then you will have to plan ahead when working the neckline of the sweater, adding or subtracting front stitches to make the back and the fronts equal. Once this has been considered and planned, work from the top down according to your pattern, increasing or decreasing any stitches on the front, until the number of front stitches equals the number of back stitches. Then join in the round after the armhole shaping is complete.

Many cardigans, when converted, will transform into a V-neck pullover. If you desire a pullover with a crewneck instead, just work the sweater from the top down until the fronts reach the bottom of your throat, or to the desired neck depth. Count the number of stitches on the back and cast on the required number of stitches between the two fronts so they equal the number of stitches on the back, join the work after the armhole shaping is complete, and work to the bottom edge. For more on changing neckline shaping, see page 142.

BOTTOM-UP PULLOVER TO CARDIGAN AND VICE VERSA

If you are changing a bottom-up pullover into a cardigan, the front stitches given in the pattern will need to be split in two at cast-on (and any extra center front stitches added if you want the fronts to overlap); you will cast on stitches for the right front first, then the back, and finally the left front. Any waist or armhole shaping will need to be worked at the same time on each front. If converting a cardigan to a pullover, you will cast on all the front stitches at once, then the back stitches. If the cardigan fronts overlap, you will need to adjust the number of stitches cast on for the front so they equal the number of back stitches. Instead of working back and forth, you will join to work in the round, working the front in one piece instead of two, and working any waist and armhole shaping at both sides of the front (and back) as you work up toward the neck. Note that you will have to split at the beginning of the armhole shaping and begin working back and forth on each piece separately.

Alteration 6: Substituting Edgings

Ribbing and bands on a sweater can make or break the look of the garment, so if you are faced with a sweater pattern with ribbings or bands that don't suit you, go ahead and change them.

The first step in switching out one ribbing for another is to count the final number of stitches on your needles when it is time to add the edge. Most ribbings and edgings are worked in multiples of stitches. For example, a 1×1 rib (knit 1, purl 1) requires a multiple of 2 stitches, and a 2×2 rib (knit 2, purl 2) requires a multiple of 4 stitches. But if you're working the piece flat, and you want to have your ribbing end as it began for a balanced, tidy look, as you would with the bottom edge of a cardigan, you'll have to add 1 or more extra stitches. For instance, if you work a 2×2 rib, and you want to begin and end with knit 2, instead of beginning with knit 2 and ending with purl 2, you will have to add 2 stitches to the end. This means that you will need to make sure that your edging has a multiple of 4 stitches (knit 2, purl 2) plus 2 extra stitches (to end with knit 2). So as you work your sweater, keep in mind the multiple of stitches you require for the edging or ribbing that you choose and work an extra increase or decrease or two to bring your stitch count to the correct multiple.

The most common edgings are 1×1 and 2×2 ribs, as they are stretchable and slightly gather the piece. This gathering effect is emphasized even more when you go down a needle size or two. Consider changing your ribbing choice to a 3×1 or 4×1 rib for a nice flat edge that doesn't roll. Seed stitch is a good choice for bands on a cardigan because it doesn't stretch. Garter stitch, where you knit all rows (or knit 1 round, purl 1 round when working circularly), is another edging that neither rolls nor stretches. Garter stitch, however, can add some thickness to your piece, so if you want your garment to appear to have a smooth line, avoid Garter stitch and choose a ribbing or band that will lie flat. If you like an edge that rolls, go with Stockinette stitch, but consider including a row of purl stitches to act as a dam to halt the roll at the desired spot.

STARTING FROM SCRATCH

If you're feeling adventurous and want to try your hand at your very own sweater without a pattern, it can be simpler than you think. The key is to figure out the number of stitches you need for the top of the garment, then forget about all the stitch counts, cast on, and go. I know, I know; most knitters would rather pull out their left toenail than deal with no stitch counts, but sometimes it's best to just get over it and plunge right in. Here are three formulas for making your own top-down raglan, top-down set-in-sleeve, and bottom-up round-yoke sweaters without a pattern. Refer to the Elements to Alter section on page 142 to add your own flair to these basic formulas.

CLASSIC TOP-DOWN
RAGLAN SWEATER FORMULA

Beginning with just one simple measurement, follow these ten steps to make a basic crewneck sweater with raglan sleeves. For more information on taking measurements, see page 15.

1 Measure the back of your neck—just from one side of your back neck to the other; don't include your shoulders. (An average measurement for a woman is between 5″ and 6″.) If you want to have a neck opening that is wider than your neck, add 1″ or more to this measurement. Keep in mind that you will likely be adding neck edging, so this will reduce the total neck opening as well. For instance, if the back of your neck is 5″ and you are adding a 1″ neck edging, and you want the neck opening (after the neck edging is worked) to fit your neck closely, you might use a measurement of 6½″ or 7″. If you are working a cardigan or a deep V-neck, the neck opening (before the neck edging is worked) should be close to your neck measurement, since a cardigan or V-neck will tend to drape wider than the actual opening when you're wearing it.

2 Multiply this measurement by your stitch gauge. Example: If the back of your neck is 5″ (and you want the neck to closely fit your neck measurement), and your stitch gauge is 5 stitches per inch, multiply the numbers: 5 × 5 = 25 stitches to CO for the Back neck. To make things a bit easier, round up to an even number, 26.

3 Now you need to figure out how many stitches to CO for the Sleeve tops. To get this number, divide the number of Back stitches by 3. So, 26 stitches ÷ 3 = 8.6. Round this number down to 8 (an even number to make things simpler).

4 We know you need 26 stitches for the Back and 8 stitches for each Sleeve top. Add 1 stitch for each Front, and you have 44 stitches total for the top of the yoke. Now, get ready to CO. Find the circular needle of your choice (24″ long would work well), and CO your 44 stitches as follows: 1 Front stitch, place marker (pm), 8 Sleeve stitches, pm, 26 Back stitches, pm, 8 Sleeve stitches, pm, 1 Front stitch.

5 On the first row, and every RS row that follows, you will increase into the stitch flanking each marker. Different types of increases will give you different looks. You can knit into the front and back of a stitch (k1-f/b), you may use a yarnover (yo), or you can make one (m1). The idea is to increase into the stitches that lie before and after each marker. With this example, you would have added a total of 8 stitches to make 52 stitches. Purl 1 WS row.

6 On your next RS row, not only will you increase into the stitches before and after each marker, you will now also begin shaping your neckline. This means you will be adding 10 stitches on each RS row. Example: K1-f/b into the first stitch on the needle, and continue across the row, working increases into the stitches flanking each of the following markers, and when you get to the last stitch on the needle, k1-f/b. Continue in this manner, increasing into the first and last stitch on the needle, plus into each stitch on either side of the markers on each RS row, and purling WS rows, until the Back section is approximately 2″ or 3″, or when the garment, when placed around your neck, reaches the bottom of your throat.

7 Count the number of stitches you have in the Back section and the number of stitches you have in the two Front sections. Subtract the number of Front stitches from the number of Back stitches to discover the number of stitches you need to CO across the Front center so the Back and Front have the same number of stitches. At the end of the next RS row, CO this number of stitches to join the Fronts, and continue knitting across the left Front to the first raglan shaping line you've created, and begin your next round. As you work in the round, on every other round, continue increasing into the stitches flanking each of the 4 markers (increasing 8 stitches every other round now), until the Sleeve portion reaches about 1″ below your underarm. (You can place stitches on waste yarn or on an extra needle or two to facilitate the trying-on part.)

8 Continue working in the round and when you reach your Sleeve stitches, remove the markers and place the Sleeve stitches on waste yarn—I prefer using waste yarn because holders stretch them too much—and continue working the Body. As you do this, you will want to place a marker at the center of each underarm to separate the Front from the Back and to mark the beginning of the round.

9 If you want to, you may add more stitches to increase the width of the Body. To do this, count the number of stitches you have on the Front and Back sections and divide this number by your gauge. Say you have 170 stitches total and your gauge is 5 stitches per

inch (170 ÷ 5 = 34″). If you don't want the sweater to be very close-fitting, add 1″ to 6″ of ease (see page 17) to your bust measurement. This will give you the chest circumference of the sweater. If you want to have a sweater that is 38″ around the bust, you will need to add an extra 4″ to the circumference of the sweater, which means you will need to add a total of 20 stitches to the Body, or 10 stitches at each underarm join. So, after you place the Sleeve stitches on waste yarn, CO the extra 10 stitches at each underarm, placing a marker at the halfway mark. Then, work in the round, adding waist shaping if desired, and whatever bottom edging you want when you get there. If your stitch count doesn't match your chosen edging or ribbing requirements, just do some stealth decreases or increases on the round before you start your edging to get to the correct multiple of stitches.

10 Place your Sleeve stitches back on your needle of choice. Work the Sleeve in the round on a 16″ circular needle (if the Sleeve is large enough) or use double-pointed needles. Join the yarn and work around to the underarm, picking up the same number of stitches you CO for the Body (if you did that), placing a marker in the center underarm, and working even in the round. If you want to do some Sleeve shaping, work decreases on either side of the marker at even intervals. Try on your Sleeve as you go, and add a bottom edging of some sort. Repeat for the other Sleeve. Finally, add some clever neckline trim.

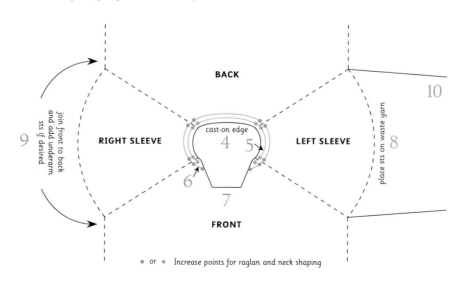

● or ● Increase points for raglan and neck shaping

CLASSIC TOP-DOWN
SET-IN SLEEVE SWEATER FORMULA

Follow these ten steps to make a garment tailored to your specifications with smooth sleeve caps that won't need to be plotted out or sewn in the traditional way.

1 Write down the following measurements: crossback, bust, armhole depth (measure the distance between the top of the shoulder and the bottom of the underarm on a favorite sweater that fits like the one you would like to make), and the back of your neck. For more information on taking measurements, see page 15.

2 Make a gauge swatch. Multiply your stitch gauge by your crossback measurement. This is how many stitches you will CO for the Back. To make it simple, round up to an even number and do a Provisional CO (see Special Techniques, page 162) for the required number of stitches. In our example, the stitch gauge will be 4 stitches per inch and the crossback is 15". So the number of stitches on the needles is 60 (15" × 4 stitches per inch = 60 stitches).

3 If you don't want the sweater to be very close-fitting, add 1" to 6" of ease (see page 17) to your bust measurement. This will give you the chest circumference of the sweater. Divide this measurement by 2 (for the Front and Back), and multiply the resulting number by your stitch gauge for the number of stitches you need for the Back (for instance, if your bust is 34", and you've added 2" of ease, then 34" + 2" = 36"; 36" ÷ 2 = 18"; 18 × 4 stitches per inch = 72 stitches for the Back after the armhole is complete). Subtract your crossback stitches (60) from the total number of stitches needed for the Back (72), and divide this number by 2 for the number of stitches you need to add to each underarm (72 total Back stitches − 60 crossback stitches = 12 total stitches to be added; 12 ÷ 2 = 6 stitches to be added to each underarm).

4 Work the Back even, without shaping, until it reaches your underarm. This is where you will begin to shape the bottom of your armhole.

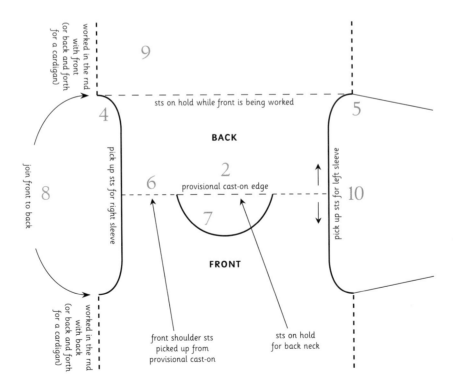

5 Shape your armhole. To do this, just work a couple of increase rows on each end of the RS of the piece and keep track of the number of stitches you need to add under each arm. Then, on your next RS row, using a Backward Loop CO (see Special Techniques, page 162), CO the remaining stitches for each underarm, on each side of the garment. Work one WS row, and carefully cut the yarn and place the stitches for the Back on waste yarn.

6 Determine how many stitches you will need for your Back neck. If your Back neck width is 5″ and you want the neck opening to be wider than your neck, you might want a neck width of 7″ (7″ × 4 stitches per inch = 28 Back neck stitches). Determine how many shoulder stitches you will have (60 crossback stitches – 28 neck stitches = 32 stitches for both shoulders ÷ 2 = 16 stitches for each shoulder). Carefully unravel the Provisional CO, and place the shoulder stitches (the first and last 16 stitches) back on your needle and the Back neck stitches on waste yarn or a stitch holder. Attach a ball of yarn and work across the first shoulder/Front. Drop your yarn, and attach another ball of yarn to the second shoulder/Front and work to the end.

7 For a crewneck with a plain band or a turtleneck, on each RS row, increase 1 stitch at each neck edge until you have added approximately ⅓ of the required center neck stitches to each edge. (That is, 28 center neck stitches ÷ 3 = 9 stitches [rounded] to be added to each side of the neck.) Then, using a Backward Loop CO, CO the remaining neck stitches for the center Front neck and join the Front pieces together. You will have added 9 stitches to each side of the neck (18 stitches total), which will give you a remainder of 10 stitches that you will need to CO for the center neck (28 − 18 = 10 stitches to add to center neck). If you have a lot of stitches to add to each side, or a small number of rows over which to add the stitches, you may need to work a number of 2- or 3-stitch COs in addition to or instead of 1-stitch increases, in order to add in all the stitches needed within the available number of rows.

8 Continue working as for the Back, and work the increases for the underarm just as you did for the Back. On the next RS row, you will join the pieces together, so place the Back stitches that are currently on hold (the Back stitches after working the armhole shaping, not the Back neck stitches) onto a spare circular needle. On the next RS row, work across the Front, place a marker for the right side, join the Front to the Back and work across the Back, place a marker for the left side and beginning of the round, and connect the Back to the other side of the Front. The garment is now all in one piece.

9 Work in the round, adding waist shaping at the markers, if desired, and work down to the bottom edge. Add an edging of your choice and BO.

10 Pick up stitches around the armholes and add the Sleeves, or for a sleeveless shell, pick up stitches around the armholes and work some ribbing for an inch. Finish the collar as desired.

CLASSIC BOTTOM-UP ROUND-YOKE SWEATER FORMULA

The most notable knitting formula of all time is for a classic round-yoke sweater and is known as EPS (Elizabeth's Percentage System). It was first published by Elizabeth Zimmermann in issue #26 of *Wool Gathering* (a 1982 Schoolhouse Press publication) and was updated in 2001 by Zimmermann's daughter, Meg Swansen, in issue #65 of *Wool Gathering*. The sleeves and body of this sweater are knitted from the bottom up, and joined at the underarm so that the yoke can be worked in one piece in the round. Following is a very basic description of how the system works, plus ideas for tweaking.

Note: For this overview, let's assume we're making a sweater with a circumference of 36".

1 Make a gauge swatch. Let's say it's 5 stitches per inch.

2 Take your measurements (see page 15). If you don't want the sweater to be very close-fitting, add 1" to 6" of ease (see page 17) to your bust measurement. This will give you the chest circumference of the sweater. Calculate how many stitches you need by multiplying your stitch gauge by this circumference (5 stitches × 36" = 180 stitches). This is your Key Number. CO your Key Number of stitches (or adjust the multiple slightly to accomodate your stitch pattern), join for working in the round, and place a beginning of round marker. *Note: If you are working a ribbed edge and want it to be fitted, subtract 10% of the Key Number and cast on that number of stitches.*

3 Work your ribbing to your desired depth, then change to Stockinette stitch and, if necessary, increase evenly to bring your stitch count up to your Key Number. Continue working until your tube reaches your armpits. You could easily tweak this step by adding some waist shaping, but when the tube reaches your armpits, you're done with the Body except for Step 4.

4 To shape the armholes, EPS suggests that 10% of the Key Number be placed on hold under each arm to be grafted to the Sleeve stitches during finishing. (In this case, 180 stitches × 10% = 18 stitches.) Starting at your beginning of round marker, work 18 stitches, then place them on waste yarn. Work to the next marker, work 18 stitches, then place them on waste yarn. *Note: My patterns direct you to bind off stitches under the arms for the Body and Sleeves, then sew these stitches together when finishing the sweater. This is an easy way to finish the underarm stitches. However, if you are comfortable with Kitchener stitch, you may prefer to place the underarm stitches on waste yarn as EPS suggests, then graft them together with the Sleeve stitches during finishing. This will result in an invisible join and a more flexible underarm. Then, place your body on an extra circular needle or a separate length of waste yarn.*

5 Sleeves come next. With the EPS system, the cuffs of the Sleeves (since you work from the bottom up) should be 20% to 25% of the Key Number. Assuming you want a traditional cuff and your sweater is snug-fitting, CO 25% (that is, 180 stitches × 25% = 45 stitches), join for working in the round, place a marker for the beginning of the round, and work in ribbing for a few inches, or however deep you want your cuff to be. Then add 2 stitches on either side of your marker at regular intervals until you reach your goal Sleeve stitch count, which should be 35% to 40% of your Key Number (that would be 180 stitches × 35% = 63 stitches), depending upon how you want the upper arm to fit. With the Sleeves, you have a ton of leeway for customization. Note that if you are working larger plus sizes, these percentages may give you a few too many stitches at the cuff. For instance, if you are working a 54" chest, 20% of that would give you a cuff circumference of 10¾", which is likely larger than you'll need. So use the percentages as a start, then tweak these numbers to better fit your own measurements.

6 Work your Sleeve up to the underarm. When your Sleeve is as long as you want it to be up to the armpit, repeat what you did with the Body and place 10% of the total Body stitches on waste yarn for the armholes. So, on your next round, work 18 stitches, place them on waste yarn, then work to the end and place the remaining Sleeve stitches on spare needles or waste yarn. Make your second sleeve in the same manner.

7 Join the pieces for the Body in the following order: Left Sleeve, Front, Right Sleeve, Back. The beginning of round marker is placed between the Back and the Left Sleeve. The yoke is then worked as a single piece to the neck. If you want to work some sort of fancy color or texture motif here, you can start anywhere you want to, really, as long as you remember to count your stitches and make necessary decreases evenly on the round before you begin the motif, so the multiple of stitches matches whatever motif you have chosen. To shape the Yoke, you will work a total of 3 decrease rounds as you work up to the neckline. Zimmermann suggests that the first decrease (a 25% decrease in stitches) be worked after ½ the total yoke depth has been knitted, then ¾ of the way up (33% decrease of stitches), then the last decrease is worked when the yoke depth has been reached (this time 40%).

8 The depth of your yoke is approximately ½ of one side of the Body, or 25% of the circumference (36" circumference × 25% = 9" Yoke depth). Keep this in mind as you work toward the top and plan motifs. Again, for some sizes, especially the larger plus sizes, this percentage will likely give you a deeper yoke than you want. For instance, if you are working a sweater with a chest measurement of 54", this percentage will have you work a yoke depth of 13 ½"; you may find that a depth of 10" is more appropriate. Try on the sweater as you go to make sure that the Yoke fits as you would like it to.

9 If you want the back of the sweater to fit more closely around the neck, work a few short rows (see Special Techniques, page 162) on the Back, between the two shoulders and just below your neck ribbing. Change to ribbing (count your stitches for the proper multiple and adjust if necessary) and work for about 1". BO all stitches, invisibly graft your underarm stitches together with Kitchener stitch (see Special Techniques, page 162) (or sew them together if you bound off stitches), and be sensational.

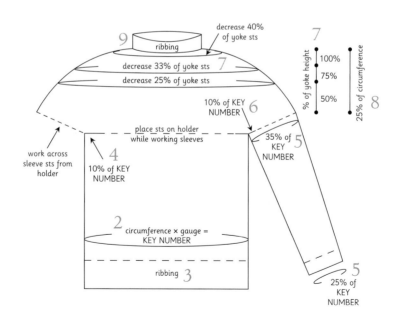

Determining How Much Yarn to Buy

For each of the main patterns in this book I tell you how much yarn you need to reproduce the results exactly. But when you are personalizing the patterns, you'll need to do some of your own calculations.

For some, this subject conjures up memories of garments gone bad—garments that were abandoned when they were almost finished because the yarn ran out. The problem with estimating yardage is that it isn't an exact science. You can come up with a close estimate, however, using a few different methods.

1 Ask your local yarn shop about the pattern and the yarn you want to use. If it is something that is familiar to them, they should be able to advise you on how much you'll need for your project. Check their return policy and buy an extra ball or two just in case.

2 Find a pattern that looks like what you want to end up with and that is in the same gauge. Compare the yardage of the yarn you want to use to the yardage of the yarn in the pattern. Multiply the number of balls in the yarn requirement in the pattern by the yardage for one ball, then from that work out how many balls of your yarn you'll need.

3 Refer to yarn requirement charts, such as Ann Budd's *The Knitter's Handy Guide to Yarn Requirements* (Interweave Press), which provide approximate yardage for garments in a broad range of sizes and gauges.

4 Calculate your yarn requirements based on the pattern's schematic. Let's say that you want to add long sleeves to a short-sleeve cardigan with a gauge of 5 rows per inch. First look at the schematic and make note of the length of the current sleeve, then note the length of the section you are adding. Next determine the width of the sleeve both at the cuff and the top of the section that you are adding. Picture each sleeve laid out flat. The basic shape of each sleeve (assuming the cuff is narrower than the top of the sleeve) is a trapezoid. If you turn one sleeve 180 degrees, and place it next to the other, you see that together they will form a parallelogram (see illustration above). To get the width of the parallelogram, simply add the width of the cuff and the width of the top of the section that you are adding. For example, if your cuff measurement is 9″ and the top of the section that you are adding is 18″, then the width will measure

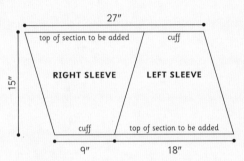

27″. Multiply the length of the section you are adding by 5 rows per inch. This will give you the total number of rows for the rectangle (15″ × 5 rows per inch = 75 rows). Since one row of Stockinette stitch takes a length of yarn approximately 3 times the width of the piece you are knitting, if you take the parallelogram as if it were one whole piece, each row that is 27″ wide will take 81″ of yarn (27″ × 3). So multiply 81″ of yarn times 75 rows for the parallelogram, and you'll get 6075″ of yarn. Divide that by 36″ to find out the yardage, and you'll arrive at 168.75 yards for both sleeves. Calculate an additional 10% or so for "padding" (185.6 yards). This method for calculating yarn will also work for adding length to a sweater or adding a collar (such as a turtleneck) that isn't called for in the pattern. If there is no shaping, you will already be working with a simple rectangle, which should make your calculations easier. If you have shaping, you may be able to divide sections into trapezoids as above. If you're uncomfortable with using this formula, use a basic rectangle instead, but know that you will likely have a lot of yarn left over—not such a bad thing!

Note: Sleeves will be worked in the round, but are pictured here as if they are worked flat, for the purpose of illustrating the calculations. The Left Sleeve is pictured after turning it 180°.

ABBREVIATIONS

BO: Bind off

Ch: Chain

Circ: Circular

CO: Cast on

Dpn: Double-pointed needle(s)

K: Knit

K2tog: Knit 2 stitches together.

K3tog: Knit 3 stitches together.

K1-f/b: Knit into front loop and back loop of same stitch to increase 1 stitch.

K1-tbl: Knit 1 stitch through the back loop, twisting the stitch.

M1 (make 1 left slanting): With the tip of the left-hand needle inserted from front to back, lift the strand between the two needles onto the left-hand needle; knit the strand through the back loop to increase 1 stitch.

M1-p (make 1 purlwise): With the tip of the left-hand needle inserted from back to front, lift the strand between the two needles onto the left-hand needle; purl the strand through the front loop to increase 1 stitch.

P: Purl

P2tog: Purl 2 stitches together.

P1-f/b: Purl into front loop and back loop of same stitch to increase 1 stitch.

Pm: Place marker

Psso (pass slipped stitch over): Pass slipped stitch on right-hand needle over the stitches indicated in the instructions, as in binding off.

Rnd: Round

RS: Right side

Sc (single crochet): Insert hook into next stitch and draw up a loop (2 loops on hook), yarn over and draw through both loops on hook.

Sm: Slip marker

Ssk (slip, slip, knit): Slip the next 2 stitches to the right-hand needle one at a time as if to knit; return them back to the left-hand needle one at a time in their new orientation; knit them together through the back loop(s).

Sssk: Same as ssk, but worked on next 3 stitches.

Ssp (slip, slip, purl): Slip the next 2 stitches to right-hand needle one at a time as if to knit; return them to the left-hand needle one at a time in their new orientation; purl them together through the back loop(s).

St(s): Stitch(es)

Tbl: Through the back loop

Tog: Together

WS: Wrong side

Wrp-t: Wrap and turn (see Short-Row Shaping, page 162)

Wyib: With yarn in back

Wyif: With yarn in front

Yo: Yarnover (see Special Techniques, page 162)

SPECIAL TECHNIQUES

Backward Loop CO: When working the CO at the end of a row, * wind yarn around thumb clockwise, insert right-hand needle into the front of the loop on the thumb, remove thumb and tighten st on needle; repeat from * for remaining sts to be CO. When working the CO at the beginning of a row, work as above, inserting left-hand needle instead of right-hand needle into the loop on the thumb.

Crochet Chain: Make a slip knot and place it on crochet hook. Holding tail end of yarn in left hand, *take hook under ball end of yarn from front to back; draw yarn on hook back through previous st on hook to form new st. Repeat from * to desired number of sts or length of chain.

I-Cord: Using a double-pointed needle (dpn), CO or pick up the required number of sts; the working yarn will be at the left-hand side of the needle. *Transfer the needle with the sts to your left hand, bring the yarn around behind the work to the right-hand side; using a second dpn, knit the sts from right to left, pulling the yarn from left to right for the first st; do not turn. Slide the sts to the opposite end of the needle; repeat from * until the I-Cord is the desired length. *Note: After a few rows, the tubular shape will become apparent.*

Attached I-Cord: Using dpn, CO the number of sts specified in the pattern. The working yarn will be at the left-hand end of needle. Transfer the needle with the sts to your left hand, bring the yarn around behind the work to the right-hand side; using a second dpn, knit the sts from right to left, pulling the yarn from left to right for the first st, pick up and knit 1 st from the edge to which the I-Cord will be attached; do not turn. *Slide the sts to the opposite end of the needle, knit to the last 2 sts, slip 2, yo, p2sso, pick up and knit 1 st from the edge; repeat from * around the entire edge to which the I-Cord is to be applied, working even knit rows between pick-ups if necessary so that the I-Cord is smooth. Fasten off.

Intarsia Colorwork Method: Use a separate length of yarn for each color section; you may wind yarn onto bobbins to make color changes easier. When changing colors, bring the new yarn up and to the right of the yarn just used and twist the yarns to prevent leaving a hole; do not carry colors not in use across the back of the work.

Kitchener Stitch: Using a blunt yarn needle, thread a length of yarn approximately 4 times the length of the section to be joined. Hold the pieces to be joined wrong sides together with the needles holding the sts parallel, both ends pointing to the right. Working from right to left, insert the yarn needle into the first st on the front needle as if to purl, pull yarn through, leaving the st on the needle; insert the yarn needle into the first st on the back needle as if to knit, pull the yarn through, leaving the st on the needle; *insert the yarn needle into the first st on the front needle as if to knit, pull the yarn through, remove the st from the needle; insert the yarn needle into the next st on the front needle as if to purl, pull the yarn through, leave the st on the needle; insert the yarn needle into the first st on the back needle as if to purl, pull the yarn through, remove the st from the needle; insert the yarn needle into the next st on the back needle as if to knit, pull the yarn through, leave the st on the needle. Repeat from *, working 3 or 4 sts at a time, then go back and adjust the tension to match the pieces being joined. When 1 st remains on each needle, cut the yarn and pass through the last 2 sts to fasten off.

Long-Tail CO: Leaving a tail with about 1″ of yarn for each st to be CO, make a slipknot in the yarn and place it on the right-hand needle, with the tail end to the front and the working end to the back. Insert the thumb and forefinger of your left hand between the strands of yarn so that the working end is around your forefinger and the tail end is around your thumb "slingshot" fashion; * insert the tip of the right-hand needle into the front loop on the thumb, hook the strand of yarn coming from the forefinger from back to front, and draw it through the loop on your thumb; remove your thumb from the loop and pull on the working yarn to tighten the new st on the right-hand needle; return your thumb and forefinger to their original positions, and repeat from * for remaining sts to be CO.

Provisional Cast-On

A provisional cast-on is used whenever you want to create a starting point in your knitting from which you can work later in the opposite direction. When you cast on provisionally, there are no seams, so I like to cast on provisionally at the top of the shoulder when working top down. This makes the tops of my shoulders look nice and smooth. *Note: For larger sizes, or when using extra heavy-weight yarn, you may find it preferable to go ahead and use a conventional cast on and pick up and knit the shoulder stitches, working your way down the front as in the pattern. This will create a seam much like a sewn-in one without disrupting the integrity of the pattern. If you like, you can hand-sew a length of binding tape at the shoulders for further reinforcement.* This technique is also helpful at the bottom of a garment to add length later. Using a provisional cast-on also comes in handy when you're not quite sure if you have enough yarn to complete a project. In the case of socks, if you use a provisional cast-on, you can work both of the feet first (from the toe up), then separate your leftover yarn into two equal balls and finish the cuffs, knowing you won't run out.

There are several ways to cast on provisionally. My favorite method is the Long-Tail Cast-On version. To do the Long-Tail Provisional Cast-On, you first need to be comfortable with the ordinary Long-Tail Cast-On (see facing page).

LONG-TAIL PROVISIONAL CAST-ON

1 Find some slippery yarn from an odd ball in your stash that is approximately the same gauge as your working yarn (that is, the yarn you are using for your project). We can call this "waste yarn." Make sure it is in a contrasting color.

2 Make a slipknot with both your working yarn and your waste yarn held together and place the slipknot onto your needle.

3 Set up for your Long-Tail Cast-On, but put the waste yarn over your thumb and the working yarn over your index finger.

4 Cast on as usual, but notice as you do this that the waste yarn makes a nice chain at the bottom of your needle. If you make a working loop (one that sits on your needle) with your waste yarn, then you've made a mistake. Cast on the number of stitches required in the pattern, but don't count the original slipknot as a stitch.

5 When you are done with your cast-on, before you cut the waste yarn, check to see that all the working yarn is looped on the needle and the waste yarn is "chained" below it.

6 Cut your waste yarn, turn your work, and begin working your stitches as called for in the pattern. When you reach the slipknot, drop it. Let it hang while you knit.

GETTING YOUR STITCHES BACK ON THE NEEDLES

1 Recall that you made a slipknot with your waste yarn and working yarn and cast on stitches from there. Place your knitting on a table with the right side facing and with the slipknot on your right.

2 Carefully untie the slipknot and begin to unravel the stitches. As you do this, you will see a loop of working yarn. That is your first stitch. Pluck out the waste yarn and place the loop of working yarn on your needle.

3 Continue across all the stitches, plucking out the waste yarn as you go. I use the other side of my circular needle or a spare needle to do this. Keep a pair of scissors nearby in case the yarn sticks so you can carefully cut the waste yarn as you move across the row.

Short-Row Shaping

Short rows are partial rows of knitting that curve or shape knitted pieces. The result is that one section has more rows than the other, but the relative length of the piece isn't affected. Although in this book I mainly use short rows to shape sleeve caps, they can also be used to shape a shoulder slope on the top of the sweater or to shape the neckline of the front of a sweater so it swoops in toward the center, creating a drapelike effect without affecting the garment's overall length.

Ladies in need of bust shaping will often use short row shaping to create a "pocket" in the front of the garment so their sweaters don't rise up in the front. To do this in top-down knitting, knit just to the chest level, or slightly above it. Work the front section to just an inch or so before the underarm (or where the fullest part of the bust is), wrap the next stitch, and turn. Work on the wrong side of the front section to an inch or so before the other underarm, wrap the next stitch and turn. Repeat this procedure, wrapping and turning a stitch about an inch closer to the center of the bust on each side (right and left) of the garment for every cup size larger than a B-cup. In other words, for a C-cup work two sets of short rows on each side of the front, for a D-cup work four sets of short rows, and so on. This isn't an exact science, but it is a guideline. After all the short rows have been completed, work one final row across all the stitches, hiding the wraps as you encounter them, and continue working either flat or in the round, according to the pattern.

To make short rows undetectable, you will want to make a smooth transition between the edge where one row is worked and the edge that has the extra row. You do this by wrapping a slipped stitch, which prevents a hole from forming when you turn and work across the other side of the piece. Knit stitches and purl stitches are treated differently.

WRAPPING KNIT STITCHES

1 Work across the piece to the place where you want to end your short row. With the yarn in back, slip the next stitch purlwise.

2 Bring the yarn between the needles to the front of the work.

3 Slip the slipped stitch back to the left-hand needle. Turn the work, and bring the yarn to the working side between the needles. One stitch is now wrapped.

4 When you have finished your short rows, you need to hide the wraps. To do this with a knit stitch, work to the wrapped stitch. Insert the right-hand needle under the wrap, knitwise, then into the wrapped stitch. Knit the two stitches together.

WRAPPING PURL STITCHES

1 Work across the piece to the place where you want to end your short row. With the yarn in front, slip the next stitch purlwise.

2 Bring the yarn between the needles to the back of the work.

3 Slip the slipped stitch back to the left-hand needle. Turn the work, and bring the yarn to the working side between the needles. One stitch is now wrapped.

4 When you have finished your short rows, you need to hide the wraps. To do this with a purl stitch, work to the wrapped stitch. Insert the right-hand needle from behind into the back loop of the wrap and place it on the left-hand needle. Purl it together with the next stitch on the left-hand needle.

Placing Stitches on Waste Yarn: Many patterns in this book instruct you to place live stitches on waste yarn, which will not distort the stitches like a holder will. Simply thread waste yarn in a contrasting color onto a tapestry needle. Then, using the threaded tapestry needle, slip each st from the needle onto the tapestry needle and thread the waste yarn through the live sts. Pull an extra several inches of yarn through the sts to be held, and cut waste yarn.

Reading Charts: Unless otherwise specified in the instructions, when working straight, read charts from right to left for RS rows, from left to right for WS rows. Row numbers are written at the beginning of each row. Numbers on the right indicate RS rows; numbers on the left indicate WS rows. When working circularly, read all rounds from right to left.

Reverse Stockinette Stitch (Rev St st): Purl on RS rows, knit on WS rows when working straight; purl every round when working circularly.

Stockinette Stitch (St st): Knit on RS rows, purl on WS rows when working straight; knit every round when working circularly.

Stranded (Fair Isle) Colorwork Method: When more than one color is used per row, carry color(s) not in use loosely across the WS of the work. Be sure to secure all colors at the beginning and end of the rows to prevent holes.

Three-Needle BO: Place the sts to be joined onto two same-size needles; hold the pieces to be joined with the RS facing each other and the needles parallel, both pointing to the right. Holding both needles in your left hand, using working yarn and a third needle the same size or one size larger, insert the third needle into the first st on the front needle, then into the first st on the back needle; knit these two sts together; * knit the next st from each needle together (2 sts on the right-hand needle); pass the first st over the second st to BO the 1 st. Repeat from * until 1 st remains on the third needle; cut yarn and fasten off.

Twisted Cord: Fold one strand (or number of strands specified in the pattern) in half and secure one end to a stationary object. Twist from the other end until the strands begin to buckle. Fold the twisted length in half and holding the ends together, allow the folded length to twist up on itself. Tie the cut end in an overhand knot to secure.

Yarnover (yo) at Beginning of a Row: If the first st is to be knit, hold the yarn to the front [in front of the needle with no sts], insert the needle into the first st to be worked, bring the yarn over the needle and knit; if the first st is to be purled, bring the yarn around the needle from front to back, then to the front (purl position) and purl. Be careful not to lose the yo; it can easily slip out of position.

Yarnover (yo) Other than at Beginning of a Row: Bring the yarn forward (to the purl position), then place it in position to work the next st. If the next st is to be knit, bring the yarn over the needle and knit; if the next st is to be purled, bring the yarn over the needle and then forward again between the needles to the purl position and purl. Work the yo in pattern on the next row unless instructed otherwise.

YARN SOURCES

ARTYARNS
39 Westmoreland Avenue
White Plains, NY 10606
(914) 428-0333
www.artyarns.com

ARAUCANIA YARNS
Distributor: K. F. I.
P.O. Box 336
315 Bayview Avenue
Amityville, NY 11701
(516) 546-3600
www.knittingfever.com

BLUE SKY ALPACAS, INC.
P.O. Box 88
Cedar, MN 55011
(763) 753-5815
(888) 460-8862
www.blueskyalpacas.com

CASCADE YARNS
P.O. Box 58168
Tukwila, WA 98138
(800) 548-1048
www.cascadeyarns.com

CHERRY TREE HILL YARN
100 Cherry Tree Hill Lane
Barton, VT 05822
(802) 525-3311
www.cherryyarn.com

CLASSIC ELITE YARNS, INC.
122 Western Avenue
Lowell, MA 01852
(978) 453-2837
www.classiceliteyarns.com

DALE OF NORWAY, INC.
4750 Shelburne Road, Suite 20
Shelburne, VT 05482
(802) 383-0132
www.dale.no

ELANN.COM, INC.
P.O. Box 1018
Point Roberts, WA 98281
(604) 952-4096
www.elann.com

ELSEBETH LAVOLD YARNS
Distributor: K. F. I.
P.O. Box 336
315 Bayview Avenue
Amityville, NY 11701
(516) 546-3600
www.knittingfever.com

GEDIFRA YARNS
Distributor: Westminster Fibers
165 Ledge Street
Nashua, NH 03060
(800) 445-9276
www.westminsterfibers.com

JO SHARP
Distributor: JCA Crafts, Inc.
35 Scales Lane
Townsend, MA 01469
(978) 597-8794
www.jcacrafts.com

KARABELLA YARNS, INC.
1201 Broadway
New York, NY 10001
(800) 550-0898
(212) 684-2665
www.karabellayarns.com

LANA GROSSA YARNS
Distributor: Muench Yarns, Inc.
1323 Scott Street
Petaluma, CA 94954
(800) 733-9276
(707) 763-9377
www.muenchyarns.com

LORNA'S LACES
4229 North Honore Street
Chicago, IL 60613
(773) 935-3803
www.lornaslaces.net

LOUET
808 Commerce Park Drive
Ogdensburg, NY 13669
(613) 925-4502
www.louet.com

MALABRIGO YARN
Wholesale info:
(786) 866-6187
www.malabrigoyarn.com

MISTI ALPACA YARNS
Misti International, Inc.
P.O. Box 2532
Glen Ellyn, IL 60138
(888) 776-9276
www.mistialpaca.com

NASHUA HANDKNITS
Distributor: Westminster Fibers
165 Ledge Street
Nashua, NH 03060
(800) 445-9276
www.westminsterfibers.com

ROWAN/RYC YARNS
Distributor: Westminster Fibers
165 Ledge Street
Nashua, NH 03060
(800) 445-9276
www.westminsterfibers.com

TAHKI/STACY CHARLES, INC.
70-30 80th Street, Building 36
Ridgewood, NY 11385
(800) 338-YARN
www.tahkistacycharles.com

TILLI TOMAS
(617) 524-3330
www.tillitomas.com

ACKNOWLEDGMENTS

I would never have been able to write this book without the patience and love I continually receive from my husband, Theron, and my daughter, Mia. I thank them for putting up with the endless stacks of notes, and piles of yarn and for all the days and nights I've spent cooped up in my studio pondering this or that. And thanks, too, to Melanie Falick for her vision and guidance; her eye for detail and good taste really made this book what it is. Liana Allday is another wonderfully skillful editor who kept me on my toes, and was a constant, happy source of support. Sue McCain, my technical editor for this book, was amazing. I don't know what I would have done without her. Thanks also to Edie Eckman for her editing help, to Meg Swansen for helping me to understand the brilliant "Elizabeth's Percentage System" (EPS) (and for allowing me to present it on page 158), and to Anna Christian for her wonderful book design.

I am thrilled with the photographs in this book, which were created by Kimball Hall, a sensationally talented photographer. Mark Auria, the stylist, brought the knitted designs to life and gave them context with his keen sense of style. I want to thank him for organizing the five-day photography shoot. He really pulled off an astonishing feat, and for that, I am grateful. Geraldine "Gigi" Shaker did the hair and makeup and made the models, Cammy Shae Kinney, Katie Savoy, and Stevie Ryan, look even more beautiful and full of life. And my friends Betty Gust and Tammy Reed helped me knit some of the garments in this book. Without their help, I think I'd still be knitting frantically.

I want to especially thank the readers of my blog, Knit and Tonic, who offered me an endless number of enthusiastic tips and so much encouragement along the way. This book literally wouldn't exist if it weren't for the readers. It was because of them that I began to design. It was because of them that knitting became what it is for me.

And above all, I want to thank Helen Cowle, my mom's mom, for showing me how to cast on, knit, purl, and bind off when I was just eight. I love you, Grandma.

WENDY BERNARD is a knitwear designer whose patterns have been published online by Knitty and Stitch Diva Studios, in the pages of *Interweave Knits* and *Knitscene* magazines, and in the book *No Sheep for You*. She credits the readers of her popular blog, Knit and Tonic (www.knitandtonic.net), which chronicles her life and her knitting, for getting her design career started.

KIMBALL HALL is a Southern California–based photographer with twenty-five years of experience working on editorial and advertising projects. Among his clients are Four Seasons Hotels, American Express, and Bank of America.

MARK AURIA is a Los Angeles–based art director and wardrobe stylist who has worked in advertising, print, and television. His most recent clients include American and European fashion magazines and the corporations Zink, Pepsi, LG, and Apple.

ADDITIONAL CREDITS:

Makeup and Hair: Geraldine Shaker for Kitten Vixen Cosmetics, Inc.
Stylist Assistant: Cena Chisom
Production Assistant: Amy Ward
Digital Technician: Sergio Ballivian
Talent: Stevie Ryan, Katie Savoy, Cammy Shae Kinney, John Ruby, Steven Thorton, Ozzie Carnan, Ernie Felts, Gunner Keeling
Wardrobe contributed by: Cosa Nostra by Jeffrey Sebelia, Voom by Joy Han, NAP, Ellie Shoes